CALLED
TO
SERVE HIM

Preparing Missionaries to Bring People to Christ

Called to serve Him
Heav'nly King of glory,
Chosen e'er to witness for his name,
Far and wide we tell the
Father's story,
Far and wide his love proclaim.

CALLED

TO
SERVE HIM

Preparing
Missionaries
to Bring
People to
Christ

ELAINE CANNON & ED J. PINEGAR

ISBN: 1-55517-341-1

10 9 8 7 6 5 4 3 2 1

Published and Distributed by:

925 North Main, Springville, UT 84663 • 801/489-4084

CFI | Publishing and Distribution Since 1986

Cedar Fort, Incorporated

CFI Distribution • CFI Books • Inside Cougar Report

Page Layout and Design by Corinne A. Bischoff
Cover Design by Lyle Mortimer
Printed in the United States of America

Our missionaries are going forth to different nations, and in Germany, Palestine, New Holland, Australia, the East Indies, and other places, the Standard of Truth has been erected; no unhallowed hand can stop the work from progressing; persecutions may rage, mobs may combine, armies may assemble, calumny may defame, but the truth of God will go forth boldly, nobly, and independent, till it has penetrated every continent, visited every clime, swept every country, and sounded in every ear, till the purposes of God shall be accomplished, and the Great Jehovah shall say the work is done.

— Joseph Smith, Jr.
March 1842

Contents

PART 4 *The Missionary and Self*

CHOICES

This is a book about choices.

That's because life is endless choices.

Take yourself, for example. Every day you must decide what time to get up, what to wear, what to eat for lunch, which task to do first — and on and on. Then when you consider that you are a Mormon by baptism and a missionary by calling (and choice), well, you are up to your eyebrows in choices.

Life needs a menu, a specific listing of options. Like the menu, all pink and shining, that you smiled over at the ice cream parlor following your baptism years ago. But this menu would show a program, floppy disc, or high tech synchronizer: books in dark, leather covers, bright colored manuals with pictures of Jesus and Joseph. Choices.

Life needs help. Or maybe it's just you that needs help with life.

Perhaps back then you ordered from the menu the Super Decadent Double Chocolate Split topped with marshmallow sauce, hot fudge, whipped cream and a red cherry. It was fun and tasted good. Then.

Today you suck an orange as you select from life's menu,

put a program disc in the computer, and go for it. McPaint. Multiclip. Word 4. Scanner.

Or maybe you flip open the dark covered book — scriptures signed by your bishopric. Options and more options. You find a chapter and verse and wonder about the meaning of the words you read — and about you having read them. But you feel good doing it.

You decide to go prepared to study class — Sunday School, Relief Society, Missionary Training Center. The colored cover pulls you inside the manual. You find the lesson. Awesome. What can the teacher make of this? You are approaching the missionary stage. You can't imagine teaching anybody anything — except how to swim, maybe.

Life used to be easy.

You could make plans that didn't have to be worked until "someday." Dreaming...you are in a white inn on Mykonos, doing Europe with a canvas bag, one pair of jeans and your best friend...vacationing in exotic places like Delhi, St. Thomas, Tetuán, Petra...skiing Utah's famous powder until spring at Alta...seeing the world-changing rubble of the Berlin Wall...eating little meals of bratwurst and cheese, hot mustard and crispy buns while casually floating down the Rhine..hiking the Tetons...sunning on the beach like a fat seal.

Now you have discovered that you don't make your marks dreaming. Or get converts for Father's kingdom.

You weren't born to loll around the lobby of the Hong Kong Peninsula. You came into the world to do something wonderful. To make a difference. To spread the good news of the gospel. To gather together God's children.

You have been born, blessed, ordained, endowed, taught and trained, and prayed over. Now you have been called to serve. Those you are to serve are God the Father; God the Son, who is Jesus Christ; and the brotherhood of man on Earth, all children of Heavenly Father.

You go forth to wherever in the world, armed with a testimony, a knowledge of the gospel, a love for people, and a caring about their future. Plus you understand the value of making the right choice at the right time in the right way. The options don't confuse you when you understand the purpose of your life as part of the grand plan for life. You know deep inside of you that you have been called to serve Him, so you make choices according to the God's system.

When life's menu with its many choices presented itself, you chose correctly. You understand Moroni 7:16:

> "For behold, the Spirit of Christ is given to every man, that he may know good from evil; wherefore, I show unto you the way to judge; for every thing which inviteth to do good, and to persuade to believe in Christ, is sent forth by the power and gift of Christ; wherefore ye may know with a perfect knowledge it is of God."

PART 1

THE MISSIONARY AND
THE CALL

1

CALLED TO SERVE HIM

Missions. The patterns are everywhere around us: we are to serve and follow those patterns throughout our lives. To accept the blessings of the gospel is to accept a call to serve a mission.

The Mission of the Lord Jesus Christ:

> "For behold, this is my work and my glory — to bring to pass the immortality and eternal life of man" (Moses 1:39).

The mission of the Church of Jesus Christ of Latter-day Saints:

> "Invite all to come unto Christ" (D&C 20:59) "and be perfected in him" (Moroni 10:32). This mission is manifested by (1) perfecting the Saints, (2) proclaiming the gospel, and (3) redeeming the dead.

The mission of every Latter-day Saint:

> "When thou art converted, strengthen thy brethren" (Luke 22:32).

> "Go ye into all the world, and preach the gospel...."

> "He that believeth and is baptized shall be saved; but he that believeth not shall be damned." (Mark 16:15).

> "Loveth thou me? Feed my sheep" (John 21:17).

1

The commission and commandments are certain. We have a call to serve our God and his children. Our first covenant at baptism begins the preparation for our life's work as we are washed clean from our sins, we become born again with a fresh start to rise above the enchanting entice-ments of the world and do something that really matters. We set about the important effort of helping in the mission of Jesus Christ. As we do this, we fulfill our sacred covenants made with him in the House of the Lord. We are willing to sacrifice all that we have for the work of the kingdom and to keep pure so that we may have his Spirit ever with us. Thus, we are guided in his work, we are strengthened in our resolve, our relationships with God and man are sweetened, and our lives and our service — our call to serve Him — are marked with love.

Tolstory, the great Russian literary figure, is credited with the poignant fable of the earnest new ruler who approached a mountain to seek out a wise man for help. Basically, the fable tells of the ruler who wanted to succeed. He did not want to waste his opportunity. He did not want to count on his own meager perspective for serving. He asked the old man, who had given much time to the study of eternal truths, the nature of God, and the needs of mankind:

"What shall I do?

"Whom shall I serve?

"When shall I begin?"

What the new ruler expected to hear was a detailed sys-tem for succeeding at the responsibility of serving in a posi-tion of authority. What he got were basic answers of truth — simple statements to be fulfilled through the devotion of a dedicated ruler.

"What to do?

"Teach truth and only truth."

Implicit in the statement is this fact: one cannot share truth unless one has it. Thus begins the personal search for truth about God's plan and the principles required to flourish under it. Then comes the testing of truth through prayer and application. Wisely, efforts to cultivate social skills necessary for the effective exchange of good and truth will bring joy to all who honestly seek them.

Do good. Do all the good you can.

But be alert to opportunities, be courageous to change mood or circumstance; and be quick to meet need with deed.

A person cannot do good if he does not first understand the needs of those about him. What is man that God is mindful of him? Why the worldwide battles about rights? Why reminders of the worth of souls? Why corrective institutions for man's inhumanity to man? Why places of higher learning? Why spiritually oriented programs for personal progress? Why family circles to define a person's heritage, traditions, potential?

"Whom do I serve?" the new ruler wanted to know.

"Serve those closest to you," the wise man advised.

The echo sounds in the hearts of the followers of Christ, "Love [help, serve, lift, comfort, teach] thy neighbor as thyself" (Matthew 19:19). Begin with self — love thyself. You are a child of God, and he knows you and loves you and sees to it that the heavens shake for your good. This is your life, your chance, your time to prepare to meet God. "Neglect not the gift that is in thee," as Paul reminded Timothy (Timothy 4:14). Then love your neighbor. Bless those closest to you. Keep widening your circle of love, concern, and willingness to help.

"When shall I begin?" The new ruler was nervous. He didn't want to make any mistakes or waste any effort or get bogged down because he was not prepared — maybe later was better than sooner!

No way. The time is now and now is all the time you have. The whole world is waiting for the proverbial sunrise. The gospel has been restored, the wrap up, before the final scenes of earth life seems to be under way. Waves of people are waiting for the Good News. Nation after nation is being set free. Gates and hearts are opening to those who are called to serve the Savior — missionaries who are people bringing people to Christ.

The mission of Tolstoy's ruler and the mission of Christ 's followers can be said to be the same. One puts a foot to the mission path of service and is richly rewarded for taking the first step — careful to note the remarkable unfolding of the view; sensitive to the perils of the adversary and his stumbling stones; consciously grateful for good days and its opportunities; deliberately docile on the stormy days that allow time for renewal of the mind and the soul's savoring of the plan of life.

Remarkable, is it not? And all so that man may grow up in the Savior, receive a fulness of the Holy Ghost, be organized according to God's laws, and be prepared to receive every needful thing (See D&C 109:15).

2

THE HOUR OF YOUR MISSION IS COME

A s a member of The Church of Jesus Christ of Latter-day Saints you have a mission to perform. It isn't someday, it's now. The hour of your mission has come!

Wherever you are, whatever plans you have made, whatever life has imposed upon you — you have a mission to perform. The formal call to serve God for a specific time, with specific training, in a specific mission field is one wonderful opportunity. But before — and after — that call to serve, there still is missionary work to be done. There will always be people around you who need to be brought unto Christ and taught the principles of change.

War has a way of interfering with our lives. Over the generations, war also has proved to be a blessing. Some who are called up to serve their country might complain about being cheated out of a mission. Others insist that the military is as fruitful a field as any other assignment. Maybe a uniform differs from formal conservative missionary attire, but underneath it all the spirit can be the same.

Those who catch the vision of being on the Lord's errand wherever they are will meet with success. One young Mormon sailor filled with the missionary spirit recognized that his time of military service was the hour of his mission. When a new recruit named Ray showed up in his unit, he invited the man to go to church with him. After the meeting, the young sailor asked Ray if he were a Mormon.

"No, I am not a Mormon," Ray replied.

"You look and seem like a Mormon. I've watched you."

"Maybe that's because I have been raised with Mormons all my life."

"And you've never been baptized?"

"No."

"Would you like to be baptized?"

"I think so," said Ray.

"How come you haven't been baptized before?"

"No one has ever asked me before," was Ray's telling reply.

The sailor with missionary zeal soon took care of this matter. Furthermore, Ray also followed the path of personal growth toward perfection and happy service to others all the rest of his life. He too recognized the hour of his mission and helped bring others to Christ.

We are the children of God with a divine destiny, foreordained to a great work. Once we realize who we are and whose errand we are on, once we are converted to the Lord and not merely convinced that the gospel is true, we will recognize each hour of our particular mission when it comes.

> Therefore, O ye that embark in the service of God, see that ye serve him with all your heart, might, mind and strength, that ye may stand blameless before God at the last day (D&C 4:2).

You should not only memorize this scripture, but also ponder and pray that you might understand it in terms of your own life. Take it deep into your soul. Once you internalized a scripture, it can begin to mold your thoughts and actions, your goals, your very life. If you believe that you have the power to serve in such a mighty way, and if you manifest that belief through action, one day you will indeed stand blameless before God.

The Lord has prepared us to do His work. Since the foundation of the world, and according to our exceeding faith and good works in premortality, we have come to the blessed assignment of being counted among the covenant people with an important responsibility:

We are to share the gospel.

We are to increase our own understanding and strengthen our personal testimony of the Lord, His will and His way, His work and His glory.

When we are converted, we are to strengthen others.

Even before we claim a full and glowing, unshakable testimony, we will meet people who understand less than we do about sacred things. As we serve others, our own faith will increase. We will then have more power to help others. We will be enhanced with the skills and spirit to teach them unto repentance and baptism.

The Lord told Thomas B. Marsh something that applies to every one of us. If you put your own name in the place of those people you read about in the thirty-first section of the Doctrine and Covenants, the scripture will become more meaningful to you. You will be helped in your understanding of your personal responsibility to recognize and act upon the "hour of your mission."

Consider these high points in Doctrine & Covenants 31:

- "Blessed are you because of your faith in my work" (v. 1).

- "Behold, you have had many afflictions...; nevertheless, I will bless you and your family" (v. 2).

- "Lift up your heart and rejoice, for *the hour of your mission is come*" (v. 3; italics added).

- "Your tongue shall be loosed, and you shall declare glad tidings of great joy to this generation" (v. 3).

- "Begin to preach from this time forth, yea, to reap in the field which is white already to be burned" (v. 4).

- "Thrust in your sickle with all your soul" (v. 5).

- "Your sins are forgiven you, and you shall be laden with sheaves upon your back" (v. 5).

- "I will open the hearts of the people, and they will receive you" (v. 7).

- "And you shall strengthen them and prepare them" (v. 8).

- "It shall be given you by the Comforter what you shall do and whither you shall go" (v. 11).

- "Pray always, lest you enter into temptation and lose your reward" (v. 12).

- "Be faithful unto the end, and lo, I am with you" (v. 13).

This motivating section of the Doctrine and Covenants ends with this sobering reminder: *"These words are not of man nor of men, but of me, even Jesus Christ, your Redeemer, by the will of the Father. Amen"* (D&C 31:13; italics added).

The power in this counsel to prospective missionaries is evident in the experiences of the hundreds of thousands of church members who have seriously set about to share the gospel and lead people to Christ within The Church of Jesus Christ of Latter-day Saints. These are urgent days. President Spencer W. Kimball some years ago described the time of this generation in this way: "We are in the last unfolding of the last unfolding" (meeting with General Authorities and general women officers of the Church, October 1978).

One mission president greeted his new Sisters and Elders assigned to his particular area with this graphic description of the urgency in the work. He said, "I have only 1,077 days left in this mission. It is not enough time. I have slept four and a half to five hours per day, at maximum, in ten days. There is no time for jet lag. But I have never felt stronger in my life, and that's because I am committed to doing the Lord's work. Full time! This is one of the great things about being called to serve a full-time mission." The president was not suggesting that his missionaries depart from the eight hours' sleep required by the *Missionary Handbook*, but rather was using his own experience to encourage and motivate the new missionaries.

One reward of such an opportunity is that when you work full-time with the Spirit of the Lord filling you, you have thrust in your sickle. But whether it's full-time or all the time, with an ongoing attitude of knowing the hour of your mission is come, you will be a good missionary! You will lead people to Christ, and then you will reap the inimitable promise of peace — your sins will be forgiven.

3

THE CALL

The idea of going on a mission comes in a variety of ways. It might be inspiration you receive during a Church study class or during a fireside when the Spirit fills you and you feel an overwhelming desire to serve your Heavenly Father and your Savior, Jesus Christ.

Perhaps it isn't anything that dramatic. Maybe you are simply following family tradition. Your parents expect it of you: they've always talked about it, and you have even saved for it since Grandpa gave you a bank for your fifth birthday.

It's a trend among your friends. Everybody is going — almost! Maybe you have had a quiet desire all of your life and knew you would do it, someday. Maybe you and your friend talked values one evening, and everything came into focus about what really counted right now — a mission.

Perhaps you are a new member of The Church of Jesus Christ of Latter-day Saints and want to give back some of what your have found in the gospel. Sharing the fullness, the truth, and the joy with others is the only way. You set life aside for a time and make plans to fill a mission — now!

Maybe you have reached that freeing time of life when the children are grown, money isn't so tight, and you have each other and good health. Now you can fill a mission *together!*

Your devotion to duty might be overwhelming, or you might have a simple feeling that a mission is on your agenda and now is the hour. Whatever the reason, you make your desire known to the Lord and the bishop. You have your interviews. You get your papers in, and you pray some more. One day the long white envelope arrives from Church headquarters, from the office of the President.

It is the call.

Part of the information in that letter is an assignment to the mission where you will serve for a certain period of time. It is an exciting time, and those who love you have eagerly awaited the news, too.

Under inspiration from God, the Prophet Joseph Smith issued a mission call to Steven Burnett and Eden Smith. This incident is of great importance to you, too. It is worth reading about:

> Verily, thus saith the Lord unto you my servant Stephen Burnett: Go ye, go ye into the world and preach the gospel to every creature that cometh under the sound of your voice.
>
> And inasmuch as you desire a companion, I will give unto you my servant Eden Smith.
>
> Wherefore, go ye and preach my gospel, whether to the north or to the south, to the east or to the west, it mattereth not, for ye cannot go amiss.
>
> Therefore, declare the things which ye have heard, and verily believe, and know to be true.
>
> Behold, this is the will of him who hath called you, your Redeemer, even Jesus Christ. Amen (D&C 80:1-5).

The scriptures are given to us to edify, strengthen, inform, and inspire. Several critically important points in this scripture are especially for you as a missionary. Understand the incredible perspective about missionary work which the Lord offered specifically to Steven Burnett but which has application to all missionaries.

1. *Go into all the world.* Every corner of the earth contains choice people waiting to hear God's truth.

2. *Teach the gospel to everyone within the sound of your voice.* The missionary never knows whom the Lord has prepared to be gathered into his fold. The missionary's duty is to teach to all, wherever he goes.

3. *Preach only the gospel of Jesus Christ.* A mission is not about teaching world events, or giving English lessons to non-English speaking people — though you may do this — or tourism, or life on *your* homefront. It is to teach the things you have heard in church, believed, and know to be true. It is to teach and testify of Christ, to bring people to Christ, to show the way to eternal life, to provide answers from the gospel for today's problems, to baptize and confirm.

4. *This is God's will.* The call to go on a mission comes from the Lord. To serve any place in his vineyard is a privilege. The field is white — indeed, the whole earth is white, ready for the harvest. Not all will accept the gospel under your influence, but there are so many waiting for truth and direction that the hours in a day aren't enough for the work. Everywhere there is someone waiting to hear the word of the the Lord. Your assignment is to that portion of the Lord's earth where you will be especially effective, where you can touch people in a way perhaps no one else can. And you will be blessed if you are willing and attentive to the Spirit. But remember this: where you go will never be as important as what you do when you get there.

The assignment to serve is important, but your call is paramount.

Sometimes spiritual confirmation of a call comes with the letter, and a warm feeling floods your soul that it is "meant to be" to serve in a certain area at a particular time for a particular reason. The joy of receiving this confirmation is magnificent and something to be desired because it is an experience of the Spirit.

Sometime a confirmation comes after the missionary is in his or her field of labor, and, suddenly, it washes over the mind and the heart that "this place at this time is right for me."

Remember, most missionaries insist that their particular field of labor is the best. Their two years, or whatever time, were the happiest and most rewarding. When you have listened to many missionaries return and report, it becomes clear that the call to serve and then serving diligently prove important factors in joy. So go wherever you are sent, but serve with all your heart, might, mind, and strength.

Every soul on this earth is important to the Lord, and every soul will have a chance to hear the gospel of Jesus Christ either here or in the hereafter. But how great will be your joy if you bring but one person to repentance in Christ! (See D&C 18:15).

Respond to the mission call with gratitude and a real awareness that it is a privilege to be on the Lord's errand, to answer his call!

4

PREPARED TO SERVE

It has always been vital to the Lord to have preaching and teaching available to those who do not already know of His divinity, of His true principles, and of His plan for life and all eternity.

Christ himself set this example. He spent forty days in the wilderness formally preparing to serve his mission. We too must be prepared to serve as missionaries either to the dead or to the living.

A remarkable event took place on 4 October 1918 at the 89th Semiannual General Conference of the Church. The terrible years of World War I were coming to an end. Many men had lost their lives, and many Saints had questions. President Joseph F. Smith himself had been seeking guidance from God regarding a number of sacred matters relevant to the times, particularly the Lord's visit to the spirits of the dead while His own body was in the tomb.

President Smith stood before the vast congregation to give his opening address and told of sacred experiences and divine communications that he had received during that past month, including just the day before, 3 October 1918. On 31 October 1918, the revelation he had received on 3 October and had spoken of in general conference the next day was submitted to the counselors in the First Presidency, the

Council of the Twelve, and the Patriarch of the Church. They accepted it unanimously as a true revelation for the Church. This information has now become Doctrine and Covenants Section 138 and is well worth close study.

President Smith told of reading and pondering the third and fourth chapters of the first epistle of Peter, including these words, "For this cause was the gospel preached also to them that are dead, that they might be judged according to men in the flesh, but live according to God in the spirit" (1 Peter 4:6). He said, "As I pondered over these things which are written, the eyes of my understanding were opened, and the Spirit of the Lord rested upon me, and I saw the hosts of the dead, both small and great.... I beheld that the faithful elders of this dispensation, when they depart from mortal life, continue their labors in the preaching of the gospel of repentance and redemption, through the sacrifice of the Only Begotten Son of God, among those who are in darkness and under the bondage of sin in the great world of the spirits of the dead" (D&C 138:11, 57).

Another passage of scriptural wisdom warms the hearts of those preparing to embark in the service of the Lord as missionaries. President Smith told of seeing the Prophet Joseph Smith, Hyrum Smith (who was his father), Brigham Young, John Taylor, Wilford Woodruff and "other choice spirits who were reserved to come forth in the fulness of times." He said, "I observed that they were also among the noble and great ones who were chosen in the beginning to be rulers in the Church of God. Even before they were born, they, with many others, received their first lessons in the world of spirits and were prepared to come forth in the due time of the Lord to labor in his vineyard for the salvation of the souls of men" (D&C 138:55-56).

It is our understanding that those of you who have been called to serve missions today are among "the many others" prepared with "first lessons" before coming to earth.

As a missionary you will labor for the repentance and

redemption of others. Consider well your preparation for such an exciting privilege and vital service. This time is the formal period set aside from your worldly life to give everything you have to Heavenly Father and to Jesus Christ. If you hold back; succumb to selfish, self-centered, prideful, or ambitious attitudes; or seek to put yourself above others in any way, you will be amiss. If you do this, you will fall! This is not what the call nor the understanding of the preparation is about.

People who are chosen will find great joy in becoming prepared to serve. This requires humility. It requires the struggle of placing oneself totally in the hands of God. "Thy will be done" is an insistent prayer. But through spiritual growth, the missionary understands that "thy will be done, O Lord" frees a person from the tangles of selfishness and misdirected activity. By earnestly seeking and then exactly following God's will, the missionary will become stronger in commitment and firmer in faith.

"Sanctify yourselves," proclaimed Joshua, "for tomorrow the Lord will do wonders among you" (Joshua 3:5).

Preparing yourself to give everything to Heavenly Father and the Savior is an ongoing effort. If you are struggling, admit this in prayer. Plead for help to do Father's will, to keep His commandments, to serve in happiness, to remain firm in patience, faith, and duty.

It will be easier for you to allow the Spirit to hone and polish yourself spirituality because you were prepared before you came to earth to do God's work. In Alma 13:3, Alma taught that the high priests of his day were "called and prepared from the foundation of the world according to the foreknowledge of God." Similarly, deep inside you is an assurance that you were indeed prepared before you came, that you are a child of God, and that you are of great worth to Him. You are expected to be perfect; therefore, you can become perfect!

God wants you to succeed in this effort because he loves you and knows what will make you happy. He needs you to succeed in your preparations because a prepared person will be more effective in helping others of His children, whom He also loves. Thus you can be an instrument in the hands of the Lord, and great will be your joy.

Many missionaries relate the incredible experience of being with an investigator and nervously crying out to the Lord for help that the investigator will not be lost, that the correct words may be spoken and the Spirit may be so full that the result will be a commitment for baptism and confirmation.

In such a tense situation, the missionary who is prepared knows that prayer works! "O Heavenly Father, please help me say what You want me to say! May this investigator, thy child also, not be turned away from Thee because of my weakness..." Then as you begin teaching and testifying, the person is now likely to believe your words because your words are spoken by the power of the Holy Ghost. In faith and devotion you are enhanced by the Spirit. Your prayers are answered. You say things you had forgotten that you knew from your earlier preparations.

You are an effective servant of God.

5

THE MISSIONARY
WANTS TO KNOW

Even as asking questions brings the responsibility of mak-ing choices based on the answer you receive, so will making choices often raise questions. You have chosen to serve the Lord wherever he will send you, and now the questions come flooding in.

Q. I'm worried about missionary technique — things like speaking ability and teaching skill. Do I have to memorize a specific approach or gospel lessons?

A. Technique is a good thing to develop, but it won't convert anybody. A missionary's attitude must call forth the Spirit that does bring about conversion.

How the missionary treats the investigator should spring from innate wholesome goodness, from Christlike caring about others. One of the great understandings found in LDS teachings is that "the worth of souls is great in the sight of God" (D&C 18:10).

What the missionary in The Church of Jesus Christ of Latter-day Saints teaches should be truth from the standard works under the direction of the mission president. The principles contained in the missionary discussions will often help the missionary teach that truth; however,

18

a marvelous part of the work is the outpouring from the Holy Ghost upon a humble, receptive missionary. So that others may be blessed, missionaries, at appropriate times, are moved upon to say things they didn't know they knew!

Q. Missionary work seems to require greater spirituality from a person involved in it. Is this the case?

A. Teilhard de Chardin declared his basic philosophy as being an understanding of the fact that we are not humans having a spiritual experience, we are spiritual beings having a human experience.

Keep that in mind. Couple it with another truth: when you go on a mission, it is not to keep your own agenda; when you go on a mission, you are on the Lord's errand.

Q. What qualities of character are important for a missionary?

A. Being a missionary is not easy. It is one of the toughest opportunities you'll ever encounter.

A missionary needs the confidence of a tightrope walker, the commitment of a marathoner, the enthusiasm of a salesman, and the courage of a mountain climber.

Since hardly anyone claims all these qualities, be comforted that a missionary can succeed with humility and closeness to the Lord as chief personal assets. Humility means teachableness — by the Spirit, by example, and by personal study. Closeness to the Lord means working according to His will.

A woman who was serving as a general officer in the women's programs of the Church wanted her family to enjoy the remarkable experience she had visiting the Liberty Jail historical site. There Joseph Smith and his companions had been kept in chains for a long, miserable period of time. He struggled with poor health and incredibly primitive conditions. He felt forgotten by God. Yet, as he cried out to Heavenly Father, marvelous things were revealed to him that have proven a blessing to all mankind.

So this good sister's young family made the trip from Salt Lake City to Liberty, Missouri, near Independence, and waited for one of the young missionaries assigned that day as a guide. She prayed for a sensitive special person to take her well-bred family through the exhibits.

When the young Elder stood before them, it was clear that he was lacking in the fine points of personal grooming. He had little social experience. He botched the English language each time he opened his mouth. She was heartsick. The children were critical and restless.

But as the missionary gently set the stage, then moved them through the visitor's center while explaining the plight of the Prophet, the family's mood changed. The Elder testified of God's hand in the events that took place during that period. He described the outpouring of marvelous truths from heaven (now found in the Doctrine and Covenants).

Restlessness vanished, and the family became enmeshed in the tragedies and miracles that happened in that jail called Liberty! The humble missionary, enhanced by the Holy Ghost, had touched their hearts in an unforgettable tour. He was on God's errand. His personal shortcomings faded in the face of great spiritual strength and enormous caring that visitors would understand Liberty Jail, Joseph the Prophet, and how evil can be thwarted by the power of God. Great good can come through willing servants on the Lord's errand.

The woman remembered to thank Heavenly Father for answering her prayer. Her family had been lifted up by the place and by the humble missionary's transformation as he served the Lord with the Spirit in him.

Q. Why am I really becoming a missionary?

A. Ask yourself some deep and important questions. Whatever your age:

- Is it because you want to get away from home — for whatever reason?
- Is it to see another part of the world? learn a new language? meet new people?
- Is it to "find yourself" before further education? after the death of a loved one? until you make up your mind about marriage?

These things are vital pursuits but not the purpose of a specific missionary call. A mission is to teach people to come unto Christ and be baptized.

A great part of a mission is the joyful satisfaction of being about "Father's business" as Jesus, age twelve, explained to his parents (Luke 2:49).

On another occasion he explained that business in this way: "For behold, this is my work and my glory — to bring to pass the immortality and eternal life of man" (Moses 1:39).

Q. I am interested in giving back some of what I have enjoyed from the Church and society. I thought a mission would be a good way to do this. Understanding this, is it fair and honest to say to others that I have been called to serve?

A. Being called is recognizing the privilege of doing God's will under the direction of those whom he has chosen to be his servants on earth in a given place and time. There are many ways to serve society and the Church. But the call to serve a mission comes to the prospective missionary from those in authority to issue it. When and where to serve is decided under inspiration from God. This comes after the person has expressed an interest in serving a full-time mission and has filled out the appropriate papers, been interviewed for personal worthiness, and declared an ability to help finance such an opportunity.

Q. Will God protect me on my mission? I have read and heard stories about missionaries being shot, having accidents, being sick, or even dying in the mission field.

A. Such tragedies come to us whether we are old or young, missionaries or not. But certainly missionaries will be blessed who keep close to the Lord by watching and praying always, following the good rules of health, obeying the commandments, keeping mission rules, using good judgement, and making choices that are wise. All will be well, and the missionary and the family will feel this comfort and strength in all circumstances.

The following words of the Lord on this subject are recorded in the Doctrine and Covenants 103:27-28: "Let no man [or woman] be afraid to lay down his life for my sake; for whoso layeth down his life for my sake shall find it again. And whoso is not willing to lay down his life for my sake is not my disciple."

PART 2

The Missionary and the Lord

6

Is Any Thing Too Hard for the Lord?

" Is any thing too hard for the Lord?" the Lord asked Abraham in regards to the promise that Sarah should have a child, even though she and Abraham were centenarians and far past child bearing years (Genesis 18:11-14). Sarah laughed within herself when she heard that prophecy, wondering that she would bear a child when they were long past the years of reproduction. When the Lord confronted them for lacking faith, Sarah grew afraid and denied that she had laughed within herself. Then the Lord said, "Nay; but thou didst laugh" (Genesis 18:14-15).

Still the Lord did as he had spoken — "For I know [Abraham], that he will command his children and his household after him, and they shall keep the way of the Lord, to do justice and judgment." Sarah did bear the child the Lord had promised these good people. It was a son whom Abraham called Isaac (Genesis 18:19; 21:1-3).

The miracle as well as the lesson of Sarah is that the Lord can accomplish whatever is to his purposes. Nothing is too hard for the Lord. Whoever is called to serve can expect miracles in this service. When the Lord's purposes are sought and understood — when the missionary, for example, is committed to bringing people to keep the way of the Lord and to do justice — he shall be blessed.

Every missionary should understand that this possibility of miraculous outpouring from heaven happens not because of the goodness or perfection of the missionary, but because God is good and great and has a plan for his children. He uses his children on earth to bless others who need to be taught, baptized and strengthened.

It is up to the missionary to put himself or herself in a position of being used — believing that nothing is too hard for the Lord.

The Lord has commanded that we do missionary work. All of us are to be engaged in saving those who need to be led unto Christ and taught the gospel. Remember that God is our ally. He has given us no commandment save he has also prepare a way for us to accomplish it (see 1 Nephi 3:7).

The Lord also said to Jeremiah, "Behold, I am the Lord, the God of all flesh: is there any thing too hard for me?" (Jeremiah 23:27).

The Lord can fulfill that which he needs accomplished, but he often works through his mortal children to do so. If we do not do his will when called upon, he will find another worthy soul through which his purposes can be met.

Look at what already has been accomplished in the face of seemingly impossible situations:

Early Church missionaries taught the gospel in Indian territories even before the Church was fully organized.

Members of the Twelve apostles in Joseph Smith's time crossed the ocean and began teaching and baptizing there as early as 1837.

They were in Tahiti in 1844.

They were in Italy — land of the Vatican — by 1850.

Hawaii, Japan, China, Samoa, New Zealand, Mexico, Tonga, France, and Germany were being proselyted while the Saints were settling Salt Lake City — replacing primitive cabins with proper housing and making plans to erect the

Salt Lake Temple, a monument to their faith that with God's help and according to His will, nothing is impossible.

You know you are not being called to serve by selling insurance, producing moving pictures, or constructing a bridge. Men and women, couples, singles, young Sisters and the nineteen-year-old Elders are called to serve the Lord by teaching his plan and his principles so that those they teach will follow his will and one day find themselves back in the presence of Heavenly Father.

President Spencer W. Kimball once spoke these thrilling words: "I am positive that the blessings of the Lord will attend every country which opens its gates to the gospel of Christ. Their blessings will flow in education, and culture, and faith, and love, like Enoch's city of Zion, which was translated, and also will become like the 200 years of peaceful habitation in this country in Nephite days. There will come prosperity to the nations, comfort and luxuries to the people, joy and peace to all recipients, and eternal life to those who accept and magnify it.

Someone gave us this:

"To walk with God, no strength is lost.

Walk on.

To talk with God, no breath is lost.

Talk on.

To wait on God, no time is lost.

Wait on."

— (*Ensign*, October 1974, p. 14.)

So wait upon the Lord, remembering always that nothing is too hard for him. Like thousands of missionaries before you, as you do his work and serve on his errand you will discover that with God's promised help, nothing will be too hard for you. Nothing!

7

THE HOLY GHOST AND
THE MISSIONARY

Every missionary needs the constant companionship of the Holy Ghost. Missionary work is the work of the Lord; without the guidance, comfort, and sustaining influence of the Holy Ghost, little can be accomplished.

The Holy Ghost is the third member of the Godhead.

He works with God the Father and God the Son, Jesus Christ. The Holy Ghost is the medium through which God operates in giving men revelations (see John 16:13; Moroni 10:5), testimonies of the gospel and of Christ (see Matthew 16:16-17; 1 Corinthians 12:3), and all other spiritual gifts (see Moroni 10:8-17).

He has power to help people on earth in special ways. He does not have a body of flesh and bone as do Heavenly Father and Jesus Christ. He has a spirit body (see D&C 130:22). If the Holy Ghost were not a personage of spirit, he could not dwell in us and be our constant comfort and companion which Christ promised (see John 14:16-17).

The Holy Ghost is bestowed upon each newly baptized person when he or she is confirmed a member of The Church of Jesus Christ of Latter-day Saints. This is done by appropriate members of the Melchizedek Priesthood who lay their hands upon the person's head and address Heavenly Father in the name of the Son (see Moroni 2:1-3). Then, through the power of the priesthood which they hold, they say to the person whom they are blessing, "Receive the Holy Ghost."

In the Doctrine and Covenants we read that a person may receive the Holy Ghost, and "it may descend upon him and not tarry with him" (D&C 130:23). This is because the person has in some way become unclean before God. The Holy Ghost cannot dwell within an unclean person.

So precious a gift is the Holy Ghost that everyone who receives it should protect that gift so that it will not depart. We keep the Holy Ghost by living purely — living by the laws irrevocably decreed in heaven before the foundations of this world upon which all such blessings are predicated (see D&C 130:20-21). If a person commits sins — if he or she is disobedient to the God's commandments — and does not repent — the heavens withdraw themselves, the Spirit of the Lord is grieved, and what was given that person shall be taken away, "for my Spirit shall not always strive with man, said the Lord of Hosts" (D&C 121:37; 1:33).

All men are entitled to the Light of Christ, but there are special gifts that come to an individual who has the Holy Ghost bestowed upon him or her and who lives worthily, cultivating the sacred gifts.

What are some of the gifts enjoyed through the companionship of the Holy Ghost?

The Holy Ghost is a revelator. Only through him can a person surely know that Jesus is the Christ, the Son of God.

The Lord has declared that "the Holy Ghost...manifesteth all things which are expedient unto the children of men" (D&C 18:18).

The Holy Ghost, even the Comforter,...showeth all things, and teacheth the peaceable things of the kingdom" (D&C 39:6; see also 8:2).

The Holy Ghost can warn of danger.

The Holy Ghost can prompt a person to know for a certainty right from wrong, truth from error — such as the validity of the Book of Mormon (see Moroni 10:3-5).

Through the power of the Holy Ghost, you can be secure from deception.

You need not be led astray if you heed the promptings of the Holy Ghost. You need not worry what you will say and how you will respond on the Lord's errand if you are moved upon by the Holy Ghost. Remember the scripture used by generations of LDS missionaries: "And when ye shall receive these things [the writings included in the Book of Mormon], I would exhort you that ye would ask God, the Eternal Father, in the name of Christ, if these things are not true; and if ye ask with a sincere heart, with real intent, having faith in Christ, he will manifest the truth of it unto you, by the power of the Holy Ghost" (Moroni 10:4).

The gift of tongues, the gift of healing, the gift of prophecy are also gifts that come to bless our lives through the power of the Holy Ghost.

The more devotedly a person adheres to God's will and completely conforms his or her life to the teachings of Jesus, the greater will be his testimony and the manifestations of the gifts.

If ever anyone needed the spiritual gifts of the Holy Ghost, it is a missionary. On those choice occasions, a deserving Elder or Sister feels the power of the Holy Ghost working in the body like a thunderbolt, an electric current, a warm and vibrating blanket, or a bath of healing fluid pouring over all the entire being. On such an occasion an indescribable joy fills the being and love permeates the soul, surpassing anything that could be felt through physical senses alone. It is a dynamic experience and cannot be denied.

There is a traditional formula that you can follow to gain a gift through the power of the Holy Ghost. First, you must have a desire. Second, study it out in your mind using the scriptures as a guide. Third, live obediently, following God's commandments for personal purity, such as being morally clean, keeping the Word of Wisdom, supporting loyally the leaders of the Church, and being honest and loving to your fellow men. Fourth:, pray to the Father in the name of the Son, and in sincerity and humility, without doubting for a witness.

It will come.

Elder Delbert L. Stapley taught an important lesson in a conference address he gave many years ago. He said, "The natural inclination of man is to rely solely upon himself and to ignore the purpose of his existence as well as his relationship to God, who is his spiritual father. If man will recognize his divine origin, he will then realize his Heavenly Father will not leave him alone to grope in darkness of mind and spirit, but will make available a power to influence him in right paths and into standards of good behavior. The Holy Ghost is that power" (*Improvement Era*, December 1966, p. 1142.)

Free agency is an eternal gift to each of us. Neither Heavenly Father nor his son Jesus Christ will force any person into obedience, into joy, or into heaven. We must seek for ourselves the blessings of the companionship of the Holy Ghost.

8

PRAYER

It was breakfast in the huge dining room of the mission home in London. The Elders, the couples, the Sister missionaries, the president and his family, and official guests from Church headquarters had knelt together in prayer and now were enjoying a simple meal to start the day. Conversation was easy because one of the guests reminded the missionaries of a "mother at home," and they responded to her queries and promptings easily.

"What have you learned lately in the mission field that is important to you?"

Each in turn gave his or her perspective. One felt broadened by travel. Several said they knew Jesus better. One had learned to organize life and time. Another was getting a handle on applying gospel principles to life situations. Several noted people growing and changing after conversion. There were many good ideas.

Then one Elder spoke in a solemn, serious manner: "I have learned that when I pray, if I don't stay on my knees until I feel different, it is like tracting with my shoes off. It doesn't last very long."

Stay on your knees until you feel different!

Pray until you know you have connected with Deity —

that your heart is contrite and humble and your mind open and receptive for God's spirit.

Prayer is our way of communicating with heaven. It is an exchange of love with Heavenly Father. It is an earth child checking in with his Heavenly Father. It is a servant seeking direction, comfort, and strength from the Master.

The first part of your prayer after calling upon Heavenly Father may be to keep very still and wait for that closeness to come upon you. Listen to your heart and reach with your mind until you feel different from when you knelt down. That's when your spirit has connected with heaven.

Recall the incident in the mission of Jesus when he was coming into Jerusalem and the crowds were pressing about him, trying to get close to him. A woman who had been diseased for twelve years felt that if she could but touch Jesus' clothing she would be made whole, so she found the hem of his garment and touched it. Jesus, even in the midst of the crowd, felt her touch His clothing. Her touch was different from the press of the crowds. She had connected in faith, and He knew it. And she was immediately healed.

That is what it means to stay on your knees until you "feel different." To spin off a memorized prayer or mumble a quick message to God is not the same as —

- Communicating in humility with God the Father in the name of his Son, Jesus
- Having an exchange of love
- Sharing deep feelings of gratitude and need
- Cleansing the soul through confession
- Pleading for forgiveness
- Witnessing your resolve to do better
- Praying for them that despitefully use you
- Asking for guidance to find people waiting to be taught

- Seeking understanding of gospel principles as recorded in the scriptures
- Promising obedience
- Explaining your need for strength to endure
- Seeking facility in a language and in learning the teaching material
- Searching for ways to love your companion and investigators
- Asking for help in setting aside the romantic pull at home
- Crying out for confidence to do God's will
- Desiring power to heal and bless
- Yearning before God for peace on earth and holiness among men
- Expressing love and thanks for the mission president and his family

The scriptures are of full of helpful counsel on prayer. A missionary really needs to know the wisdom in daily personal prayer, the miracle in group prayer, the strength and learning in urgent prayer, the growth and sense of well-being in prayers of gratitude. In today's world of disease and impurities, a prayer upon the food that it may be blessed by God is important. Ask God to bless the food that it will be for the good of your body, that what you eat may be pure and sweet and strengthening, and that it is accepted it in gratitude in a world of starving multitudes.

The scriptures have this to say about prayer:

> Pray always, lest ye enter into temptation and lose your reward (D&C 31:12).

> You must study it out in your mind; then you must ask me if it be right, and if it is right I will cause that your bosom shall burn within you (D&C 9:8).

Pray always, that you may come off conqueror (D&C 10:5).

Pray always, and I will pour out my spirit upon you (D&C 19:38).

The prayers of the faithful shall be heard, and all those who have dwindled in unbelief shall not be forgotten (2 Nephi 26:15).

Pray unto the Father with all energy of heart (Moroni 7:48).

Love endureth by diligence unto prayer. (Moroni 8:26).

If any of you lack wisdom, let him ask of God, that giveth to all men liberally, and upbraideth not; and it shall be given him.

But let him ask in faith, nothing wavering. For he that wavereth is like a wave of the sea driven with the wind and tossed (James 1:5-6).

Be thou humble; and the Lord thy God shall lead thee by the hand, and give thee answer to thy prayers (D&C 112:10).

Draw near unto me and I will draw near unto you; seek me diligently and ye shall find me; ask, and ye shall receive; knock, and it shall be opened unto you (D&C 88:63,64).

Many people think of chapter 34 of Alma as the definitive statement concerning this life — it is the time to prepare to meet God. The notes at the beginning of the chapter seem to concur. However, it is interesting to note that much of this chapter has to do with prayer and the way to communicate with God before actually meeting him. Read again this exciting scripture and note particularly — because of our discussion here about prayer — verses 17 through 27. Take heed!

9

SPIRITUALITY

The two young missionaries kept an appointment with a fine gentleman who was an avid student of the Bible and quoted chapter and verse readily on almost any subject. This was the third time back to teach him, and the Elders were excited that this would be the time the man would commit to baptism.

When missionaries arrived at the scholar's home they were disappointed to find that a member of a prominent proselyting evangelist church had been invited to come. The four sat about the room for a time, each with his scriptures open. The investigator had many questions. The evangelist arrogantly took over the discussion, and the young men became targets for questions and ridicule from the evangelist. They were no match for the older men when it came to ready knowledge of the points of the Bible. However, they honored their calls to serve as missionaries and felt deeply about the Lord Jesus Christ, wanting to do his will. They had prayed sincerely before this appointment because they earnestly wanted to bring their Bible scholar friend to the truth.

They tried to turn the conversation from the Bible to the Book of Mormon, but the two would not be budged from biblical comparisons.

As the study session continued, contention began to

mount. The evangelist became highly agitated. The investigator, who had welcomed the young missionaries so warmly, now seemed confused and distant. A dark pall engulfed the room. The missionaries were heartsick, frightened by the growing presence of the adversary.

"Let us pray together," one of the missionaries suggested.

The idea was seized upon by the investigator, and he immediately turned to the evangelist and asked him to pray. It was disappointing to the Elders who had counted on their faithful petitions before the Lord to banish the evil atmosphere and give an opening for them to explain the gospel truth. But during the words of the evangelist the negative influences crowded the room further until it was oppressive to the missionaries. The junior companion, Elder Anderson, was frightened, too, realizing he didn't know what either of the older men knew about the scriptures. But as he struggled within himself he silently cried out to Heavenly Father. His feelings, now surging to the surface, spilled out about why he had come on a mission — to share truth, to bring people to Christ! It was not to argue over biblical interpretations, but to change lives and do God's will. He humbly asked God's help beyond their natural ability so that this fine investigator would recognize truth and that the sweet spirit of the Lord would replace the dark mood of error plaguing them now.

Strength filled his being. He was no longer afraid.

As soon as the evangelist had finished praying, Elder Anderson spoke up, suggesting that the missionaries now would like a turn to pray and asked that all kneel in a circle. His humble but fervent prayer of love for the investigator, for the Lord, and for the fulness and beauty of His gospel silenced the mumblings of the evangelist. The missionary prayed that the spirit of truth and love would enter their hearts.

Soon the mood changed. The short prayer had been answered!

The evangelist was incredibly angry and stormed out of

the house. But the investigator was so moved upon by the Spirit that tears ran down his cheeks, his heart pounded, and he witnessed that he knew the missionaries had indeed brought him the true way to worship God and live his life.

A missionary needs to cultivate spirituality.

The Spirit can prompt people to receive truth. It can inspire what should be said and done. The missionary has the responsibility to desire to be worked upon by the Spirit. Put yourself in a position to receive guidance from God. Insights can be gained into the needs of those you teach so that you can make the approach that will benefit them.

The Spirit can open doors, and the honest in heart will trust you to give them truth:

> Behold, I will go before you and be your rearward; and I will be in your midst, and you shall not be confounded. (D&C 49:27).

> And again, I will visit and soften their hearts, many of them for your good, that ye may find grace in their eyes, that they may come to the light of truth, and the Gentiles to the exaltation or lifting up of Zion (D&C 124:9).

> And if thou wilt inquire, thou shalt know mysteries;...that thou mayest bring many to the knowledge of the truth, yea, convince them of the error of their ways. (D&C 6:11).

The Spirit can generate feelings of charity, which is the pure love of Christ. The second great commandment — to love your neighbor as yourself — can become a reality for the missionary. Respect and concern can be softened into real godlike affection as you yearn and pray over the people you teach.

Paul was one of the most effective, most powerful missionaries following Christ's mission on earth. He effectively taught gospel truths and motivated people to change lives.

He loved the saints with whom he worked. He yearned for those who were investigating the gospel. He reminded the missionaries sharing the gospel of Jesus Christ of the importance that their attitude and behavior reflected the pure love of Christ. His writings on charity have become a kind of creed for today's missionaries, as well:

> Though I speak with the tongues of men and of angels, and have not charity, I am become as sounding brass, or a tinkling cymbal.
>
> And though I have the gift of prophecy, and understand all mysteries, and all knowledge; and though I have all faith, so that I could remove mountains, and have not charity, I am nothing.
>
> And though I bestow all my goods to feed the poor, and though I give my body to be burned, and have not charity, it profiteth me nothing.
>
> Charity suffereth long, and is kind; charity envieth not; charity vaunteth not itself, is not puffed up.
>
> Doth not behave itself unseemly, seeketh not her own, is not easily provoked, thinketh no evil;
>
> Rejoiceth not in iniquity, but rejoiceth in the truth;
>
> Beareth all things, believeth all things, hopeth all things, endureth all things.
>
> Charity never faileth....
>
> And now abideth faith, hope, charity, these three; but the greatest of these is charity.
>
> — 1 Corinthians 13:1-8, 13

When missionaries develop true spiritual closeness to God, it indicates that they are thinking on the level and will of God, they have conformed their lives to the Lord's standards, they have studied the scriptures to learn of the Lord and to feel close to him, and they have examined their work and their actions, repented, and cried out in prayer for forgiveness.

And they have felt a flood of love and concern for the people with whom they work as missionaries for the Lord Jesus Christ. Do you recall the remarkable words of Alma in which he states that the Lord grants unto all nations, of their own nation and tongue, to teach his word and all that is just and true? Then Alma the great missionary says, "I know that which the Lord hath commanded me, and I glory in it. I do not glory in myself, but I glory in that which the Lord hath commanded me; yea, and this is my glory, that perhaps I may be an instrument in the hands of God to bring some soul to repentance; and this is my joy" (Alma 29:8-9).

Alma talked with his son Helaman about missionary work in a way that surely expresses what everyone who works to bring people to Christ should feel: "...I have labored without ceasing, that I might bring souls unto repentance; that I might bring them to taste of the exceeding joy of which I did taste; that they might also be born of God, and be filled with the Holy Ghost. Yea, and now behold, O my son, the Lord doth give me exceedingly great joy in the fruit of my labors..." (Alma 36:24-25).

Paul is famous for his epistles. The way he taught the gospel through writing and speaking converted even his servant Onesimus.

He wrote phrases like "dearly beloved, and fellow laborer"; "Grace to you, and peace, from God our Father and the Lord Jesus Christ. I thank my God, making mention of thee always in my prayers" (Philemon 1:3-4). He also wrote: "We then that are strong ought to bear the infirmities of the weak, and not to please ourselves. Let everyone of us please his neighbor for his good to edification" (Romans 15:1-2).

What if missionaries were so spiritually mature, so filled with God's power that they wrote phrases like that to investigators and family members?

What if missionaries were so filled with the Spirit that they not only testified that Jesus is the Christ, but did so in special strength and power?

Cultivate spirituality that you may enjoy the choice satisfaction of being close to the Lord and witness the great good that can come into the lives of others.

The following scripture is pertinent: "Behold, there are many called, but few are chosen. And why are they not chosen? Because their hearts are set so much upon the things of this world, and aspire to the honors of men, that they do not learn this one lesson: ...that the powers of heaven cannot be controlled nor handled only upon the principles of righteousness" (D&C 121:34-36).

10

DISCIPLES OF CHRIST

The joy of missionary work will become yours as you become a true disciple of Christ. You receive joy when you know that what you are doing is meaningful, important, needed, and appreciated. The greatest joy of all comes when you are doing the will of the Father. You'll see!

How quickly God's work and will is accomplished depends upon a corps of servants who know how to spread truth, who are willing to fight wickedness, who are valiant and will stand firm in the faith under all circumstances, who are prepared to fill assignments and accomplish much good.

It depends on the efforts and examples of people devoted to being true disciples.

"Apostolic ministers chosen to labor among the Jews, and also those who rendered similar service among the Nephites, are called the *'twelve disciples'* (Matt. 20:17; 3 Nephi 19:4)" (Bruce R. McConkie, *Mormon Doctrine*, 2nd ed. [Salt Lake City: Bookcraft,1966], p. 198).

The dictionary defines *disciple* as "one who subscribes to the teachings of a master and assists in spreading them; an active adherent, as of a movement or philosophy" *(The American Heritage Dictionary,* Second College Edition [Boston Houghton Mifflin, 1985], p. 402).

By this standard, all the prophets who have lived, beginning with Adam, have been disciples of Christ — Adam, Noah, Abraham, Isaac, Jacob, Lehi, Nephi, Alma, Joseph Smith and so on.

Faithful members of the church are followers after Christ and want to help further his work. However, having all the discipline and character traits of Jesus Christ, the only perfect being to live on earth, is another matter. We need to struggle for the goodness, the mercy, the compassion, the joyful demeanor, and the loving and hopeful nature of the Lord. A true disciple is a learner and is not easily wearied in growing in understanding and performance of God's ways and will.

A missionary in The Church of Jesus Christ of Latter-day Saints today can and should aspire to the descriptive phrase, honorable title, and coveted quality of character of "disciple of Christ."

A true disciple believes all the doctrines of Christ as He taught them (Ether 4:10-12).

A true disciple makes a valiant effort to obey all the principles of Christ's gospel.

A true disciple reflects the mighty change in heart that results from living close to the Savior (Alma 5:13-14).

A true disciple assists in the work of bringing forth righteousness and love among God's children.

Here is a stunner statement: "Let no man be afraid to lay down his life for my sake; for whoso layeth down his life for my sake shall find it again. And *whoso is not willing to lay down his life for my sake is not my disciple*" (D&C 130:27-28; italics added).

In every dispensation God's children have been sorely tried. Remember Moses and the children of Israel in the wilderness following their years of slavery. Remember Lehi and his family who left the comforts and wealth of Jerusalem for the frightening trip across the waters in "homemade" vessels! Remember the inquisitions. Remember the witch hunts during time of the Pilgrims. Remember the Saints in the early days of the Church and the persecution, the many moves, the heartbreaking martyrdom of Joseph and Hyrum. Early missionaries went without purse or scrip and labored under difficult circumstances and personal deprivation. There is no comparison to the advantages that today's missionaries have!

Today it is at once easier and more demanding to be a proselyting missionary and a disciple of Christ. The forces of Satan are working incredibly tirelessly and cleverly to thwart the holy work of God. Greater are the temptations and trials, but more successful is the work when disciples of Christ of any age and either gender put their shoulders to the wheel to gather souls before God.

What has the Lord said people must do to prove themselves as his disciples? In the Doctrine and Covenants 59:1-9, the following ideas are expressed on this subject:

- Maintaining complete and total dedication to the work
- Keeping an eye single to the glory of God
- Having faith and diligence
- Obeying the gospel
- Loving the Lord with all our heart, might, mind, and strength
- Serving the Father in the name of the Son
- Thanking the Lord in all things
- Offering up a sacrifice unto the Lord in righteousness
- Having a broken heart and a contrite spirit
- Keeping unspotted from the world
- Going to the house of prayer and offering up our sacraments upon the Lord's holy day

The restrictions of obedience and whole-soul dedication often seem difficult. But sweetness follows the works of such righteousness; our promised reward is "peace in this world, and eternal life in the world to come" (D&C 59:23).

Any person alive to the stress of our day welcomes such a reward.

There will come a time and a place when those who have embarked in the service of the Lord will be called upon to return and report — to give an accounting of their missionary service. There is a place on earth and a place in heaven for the steward to delineate his efforts. This is a fact. It's the Lord's work, and it will be handled according to the Lord's will. Our part in it will prove our discipleship.

The following statements by great missionaries have been gathered as an inspiration for those who have been called to serve today:

Brigham Young: "When men enjoy the spirit of their missions and realize their calling and standing before the Lord and the people, it constitutes the happiest portions of their lives" (in *Journal of Discourses* 8:53).

Melvin J. Ballard: "No missionary who has performed his or her duty feels to regret the sacrifices that have been made. Joy such as is not known in any other work comes to them, and there comes too a personal development that will be of benefit to them no matter what their future occupations may be....

"I can speak from knowledge — that there is no joy equal to that which comes to the man or woman who is performing missionary labor. I would not exchange the joy that has come to me out of those fourteen years for millions of dollars. God bless the men and women of Zion that they may continue to give themselves and their means freely to this cause and participate in the supreme joy that comes from bringing souls unto Christ, and lay a foundation for eternal dividends of joy and happiness in association throughout eternities that are to come with those to whom we have been the instruments in bringing the light of knowledge and truth" *Improvement Era,* May 1930, p. 486).

George Albert Smith: "We spend most of our time, many of us, seeking the things of this life that we will be compelled to leave when we go from here, yet there are the immortal souls around us whom, if we would, we could teach and inspire to investigate the truth and implant in their hearts a knowledge that God lives. What treasure in all the world could be so precious to us, for we would have their gratitude here and their everlasting and eternal appreciation in the world to come" (in Daniel H. Ludlow, ed., *Latter-day Prophets Speak* [Salt Lake City: Bookcraft, 1948], p. 394).

Heber J. Grant: "I feel sorry for the man or the woman who has never experienced the sweet joy which comes to the missionary who proclaims the gospel of Jesus Christ, who brings honest souls to a knowledge of the truth, and who hears the expressions of gratitude and thanksgiving that come from the hearts of those who have been brought by his labor to a comprehension of life eternal" (in Ludlow, *Latter-day Prophets*, p. 395).

Nathan Elder Tanner: "Sacrifice means going without or giving up something which is good for something which is better (as quoted in Theodore M. Burton, "Testimony — a Motivating Force, *Improvement Era,* December 1962, p. 933). Such is the case as a person responds to a call to missionary service.

Being a disciple of Christ means being willing to live the law of sacrifice — to give all that you have, including life itself — for the kingdom and the cause. Missionaries are seldom in the field very long before they realize they have ample opportunity to be a disciple — to sacrifice.

Christ gave his all for us that we may be cleansed from sin and suffering. He has asked that missionaries do a valiant service for Him. Think of Christ on the cross: think of Christ bleeding at every pore in inconceivable suffering.

Then think about changing your life, learning to speak up as a witness, being willing to help others, trying diligently to keep mission rules in spirit and in deed. It can be done, for with Christ nothing is impossible, and He will help the missionary to perform appropriately and meet success in unexpected places.

This is some of what it means to be a disciple of Christ.

For a view of what can happen when people become warring, waning in obedience, and wicked, study this well: "Peace did remain for the space for about four years, that there was no bloodshed. But wickedness did prevail upon the face of the whole land, insomuch that the Lord did take away his beloved disciples, and the work of miracles and of healing did cease because of the iniquity of the people. And there were no gifts from the Lord, and the Holy Ghost did not come upon any, because of their wickedness and unbelief" (Mormon 1:12-14).

11

THE LORD'S
INSTRUMENT

Every day except Sunday, a certain faithful Latter-day Saint did dental work. It was how he earned his tithing, he explained, and was entirely a satisfying and rewarding profession. Often he would go to the hospital to perform oral surgery, usually on the third molar, known as the wisdom tooth.

The oral surgeon and his anesthesiologist would dress in surgical suits. The patient would be "bagged"; that is, breathing would be done for him by a machine. The tracheal tube would be in place; the mouth would be gagged; the eyes would be closed and covered.

As the surgery would begin, this good man would put out his hand and request the instrument he needed at each step along the way to help him accomplish the corrective surgery: "Periosteal elevator," "scalpel," and so on. He would make the incision in back of the second molar and obliquely past it. Then he'd remove top tissue and begin to do the surgery.

The scalpel in his hand was the instrument of his work. He was the master. It did whatever he told it to do and did it well. The instrument was positively clean. The instrument was sharp. The instrument filled its duty. The instrument, with the help of a dedicated and skilled expert, accomplished the purpose for which it was engineered.

So it is with the missionary who is placed in the position of being an instrument in the hands of the Lord to accomplish his holy work.

As a missionary you need to be submissive, meek, lowly, humble, brokenhearted, contrite. These are the conditions of character that the Lord can best work with. As you give yourself to the Lord, as you let him use you as he will, as you succumb to his will, you will accomplish a greater good than ever you could do alone.

As a missionary, you will have times when you will be influenced by the Holy Spirit when you write or speak. You might write words you don't recognize and say words you didn't know you knew. You will silently marvel at the privilege of knowing that you are being especially blessed for the Lord's purposes. People will believe your words because you will give them by the power of the Holy Ghost. You must be pure and positively clean; you must be sharp in your preparation, communication skills, and gospel knowledge.

Look to the sons of Mosiah for an example of how to become spirited, effective servants of the Lord. The sons of Mosiah — Ammon, Omner, Himni and Aaron — had repented from worldliness and had filled miraculous missions for the Lord. This moving story is recorded in Alma 17-26. These young men waxed strong in the knowledge of the truth. They were men of sound understanding. They had searched the scriptures diligently so that they might know the word of God. They taught with power and authority because they had followed the steps to conversion and had received the personal revelation that Jesus is the Christ!

You, too, can be perfect instruments that teach with the power and authority of God, with the spirit enhancing your personal preparations.

This is what the Lord expects of you, and what the Lord expects you can do (1 Nephi 3:7). In the strength of the Lord you can do all things. He does not leave you unattended. He wants you to succeed at this work. You are important to him.

The work is important to him because it supports his mission to "bring to pass the immortality and eternal life of man" (Moses 1:39). He knows and wants to save all people of accountable age.

To qualify for the kinds of blessings in your labors that the sons of Mosiah and all great missionaries have enjoyed—

1. *Vow to keep your life clean and worthy.* Avoid the sins and the time-wasting activities of the world.

2. *Don't be illiterate in the gospel.* You can't teach what you don't know. You won't feel what you aren't conditioned to feel. Learn from the scriptures, from the conference addresses of the Church leaders, and from the opportunities that Church programs provide. Learn, study, and pray in faith for understanding. Missionary work *is* important! As the faint stirrings come inside you to heed the call to serve a mission, you'll want to focus your reading and your listening in Church situations, to grow in the gospel. You'll want to engage in conversations that will lift your spirit and enliven your mind. And you'll desperately want to talk to Heavenly Father.

3. *Mind your money.* Financial preparation is necessary. If you finance your own mission as far as possible, you will appreciate the experience more. This is your mission, your sacrifice, and the resulting blessings will be yours to enjoy.

4. *Seek to gain a strong testimony.* A true testimony comes through the power of the Holy Ghost, a gift given you from God. You need to desire the gift. You need to study the word of God. You need to live in humility and cleanliness to earn the incredible confirmation of truth about sacred things.

Pray earnestly for this gift. Desire the wondrous confidence, enrichment and sweet comfort of knowing :

- Jesus is the Christ.
- You are a child of God the Heavenly Father.
- The Book of Mormon is true.
- Joseph Smith was a true prophet through whom God restore the gospel.

5. *Reevaluate your life.* Can you measure up to being a child of God, with the spark of the divine in you? Are you good at being a son or daughter of God — or are you only good at golf, grandchildren, dating, travel, interior design, or your particular hobby. What are you doing to help in the work of the kingdom? What will you be able to take with you if you were to die tomorrow — or be called to serve?

6. *Stretch your soul.* Be a "no limit" person in terms of your dreams and goals and talents and God's will. Consider the quality of your personal investment in the lives of others. Improve your household and community. Develop ears that hear, eyes that see, and hearts that heed the things of God.

One day it will be your turn to be an instrument God's hands to accomplish a small or great good and bring great joy to someone who needs closeness to the Lord and truth in his or her life.

12

BE VALIANT TO THE LORD JESUS CHRIST!

T he purpose of missionary work is to bring people to Christ and to help them understand the importance of being valiant to him. Since you cannot teach what you do not yourself know, it is vital for you to consider who the Lord is.

What do you think of Christ?

Do you know Him? Have you enjoyed His redeeming love? Have you suffered distress as you felt withdrawn from Him as a sinner? Trying to be more valiant to Christ includes turning away from worldly and weak ways and yielding your heart to the Lord. When you do so, a miracle happens. You are filled with warmth and a sweet stirring of the soul. You want never again to be without such a feeling.

Who is this Christ that when you turn to him you feel great love from him and you know that he cares about you?

Who is this Jesus Christ?

He is the Son of God, the Only Begotten of Heavenly Father in the flesh. He is the Son of God and the Son of Mary on earth.

He is the needful Redeemer and Savior of all the world, according to the plan of life prepared for us by God our Heavenly Father.

He is the center core of the gospel that every missionary

teaches and the members of the Church of Jesus Christ try valiantly to adhere to.

He is the head of this Church and has called leaders and prophets to guide affairs.

In Christ all things are fulfilled. Life as Heavenly Father intended must be founded on our faith in Christ, repentance through Jesus Christ, baptism and taking upon oneself the name of Jesus Christ, and receiving the Holy Ghost as a gift from Jesus Christ.

Christ means "anointed one."

Christ is the atoning one.

He came to do the will of Heavenly Father and draw all men back into the presence of the Father.

Consider examples from the Savior's life in your effort to remain valiant, loyal, and an enthusiastic servant called by him to help in the sacred mission of helping mankind.

Think of the redeeming love you feel when you are keeping his commandments and drawing close to him. He shares his love and his light. He sacrificed his life — he chose to drink that bitter cup for us. He turned the other cheek. He forgave his enemies.

How do you measure yourself against Christ? What kind of life are you living in the reflection of his life and light. How valiant are you?

The Prophet Joseph Smith reminded the Saints, "No man can be a minister of Jesus Christ except he has the testimony of Jesus" (Teachings of the Prophet Joseph Smith, sel. Joseph Fielding Smith [Salt Lake City: Deseret Book Co., 1938], p. 160).

The way to get a testimony is to study the gospel and the life of Jesus Christ. Pray to see if these things are true. Pray earnestly to know that the Lord and Heavenly Father know you are praying for a testimony! Apply gospel truth to life's situations and keep the commandments. "Experiment upon the word," and see that the gospel is the way to happiness.

When you feel the spirit fill you and you are a witness to the wonders of the Lord's way; when you have proof within you of the truthfulness of the living Christ, of the validity of the gospel, of the restoration of the gospel, and of the truth of Book of Mormon; when you have a testimony of all these things — then with power and with valor you will desire with all the energy of your soul to witness to others of these sacred things.

PART 3

THE MISSIONARY AND
THE WORK

13

PROCLAIM THE TRUTH

T he Lord God speaks to you!

> Hearken, O ye who have given your names to go forth to proclaim my gospel, and to prune my vineyard.

> Behold, I say unto you that it is my will that you should go forth and not tarry, neither be idle but labor with your might —

> Lifting up your voices as with the sound of a trump, proclaiming the truth according to the revelations and commandments which I have given you.

> And thus, if ye are faithful ye shall be laden with many sheaves, and crowned with honor, and glory, and immortality, and eternal life (D&C 72:2-5).

There are certain phrases in the Lord's proclamation that you should understand and remember.

To you who have given your names to be missionaries the Lord has said, "Hearken!" This means to listen very carefully, to pay close attention and heed his voice. He wants you to get the meaning of what he is saying, for your actions will depend on your understanding of his word and will.

Then he says that it is his will that you not tarry. In other words don't sleep away the hours, resisting the assignment.

Don't knock about town, dally in the mall, check out the fast food places, or window shop. Or whatever else you may encounter that is really unimportant and may interfere with the Lord's work.

It is not part of the Lord's will that you be idle: "Neither be idle!" Forget about giving in to laziness and procrastination. Don't fill your time with "make work" projects that fill the hours but are far removed from teaching people the gospel.

"Lift your voices!" says the Lord. Speak like the sound of a trump that announces or proclaims or dares to share good news. Uncertain trumpets are not taken seriously. Remember that you are on the Lord's errand and guided by him. All will be well. Confidence and a certain trump quality to your preaching and teaching will make you believable to the people whom God loves enough to lead to you to be taught his gospel.

In this same section the Lord also counsels missionaries to call on the name of the Lord for the Comforter, which shall teach you all things that are expedient for you to know, and to pray always that you faint not. If you do this, he promises to be with you even unto the end (see D&C 17:10-12).

What more could a traveling teacher of the most important truth on earth ask than to be taught by the Comforter and to be strengthened to the end?

It remains only that the teacher follow the Lord's counsel and feel deep gratitude for such a privilege as having the Lord mindful of every move he or she makes.

The following five steps summarize the thrust of missionary work:

1. Function properly and obediently, as Doctrine and Covenants 75 suggests.

2. Be productive. Use your time and efforts wisely.

3. Make yourself heard. Develop good communication skills. At the least, open your mouth and speak.

4. Testify with power that comes from a converted heart.

5. Perfect your performance according to a high standard of excellence. Anybody can be ordinary, but doing the Lord's work requires the best that He knows is in you!

Remember, you go into the field to baptize, not just to warn or make friends. Your goal is to bring people to Christ and proclaim the truth. Nothing more, nothing less.

14

GOLDEN MOMENTS

Two or three years maximum is all you can count on to enjoy this particular mission. To be able to serve the Lord full-time, to feel blessed and strengthened by Him at this time of your life is incredible. And there are thousands and thousands more like you taking this opportunity, too. Add families, friends, ward circle, professional and social groups, and your personal medical helpers, and you have a community of interested on-lookers.

All for you! What a boost for you while you try to bless others' lives. It is a golden chain of service and binds this period of service as a time of happiness and a sense of well-being. There will be golden moments that come as the call to serve unfolds.

Every moment of a mission is precious — the hard times, the busy, busy challenging days, the low, discouraging hours. But realizing that every moment counts puts a seal on the experience. It becomes, as thousands of returning missionaries have testified over the years, the best two years of your life to that point.

The golden moment is perishable unless you look to it and value its possibilities. Everyone is given 24 hours a day. How many golden moments you have in that time frame depends on whether time is valued and used or wasted and gone.

It only takes a moment to ask a question about the gospel, to commit someone to baptism, to lift the hands that hang down, the spirits that sag, the hopeless hearts. You can take more time than that, but a moment of thoughtful action starts a wonderful chain of possibilities.

A golden moment includes a prayerful thought as your companion is explaining a principle to the investigator ("O Father, bless Brother Brown that he will understand this doctrine." "O Heavenly Father, help Sister Lakesly that she may experience the joy of the gospel!"). A golden moment happens with a kind word, a kind deed, a smile, going twenty minutes early to church to be there to greet everybody, a longer time with the scriptures. Compliment your companion and listen to his or her presentations with open interest, even admiration. Offer what comfort you can when homesickness rages, and give consolation when disappointment hits.

Some people generate golden moments almost naturally. Consider the experience of Henry David Thoreau. Thoreau, you may recall, went to the woods alone to "live deliberately," seeking closeness to nature and peace of soul. Some of the great reflections on the value of nature and life come to us from his experience. "It is something to be able to paint a particular picture, or carve a statue and make a few objects beautiful; but it is far more glorious to carve and paint the very atmosphere and medium through which we look — to affect the quality of the day. That is the highest of arts."

Every missionary has a call to serve the Lord. Consider, too, the "other" call to serve people by changing the "quality of the day." This is the art of serving. One sister missionary told of being treated with sullen gruffness as she registered with a female clerk in a public building. Immediately the sister missionary murmured to herself that this unpleasant woman was a child of God, a soul valuable in his sight. She noticed her handwriting — clearly formed letters and well spaced lines. Neat. Legible. The missionary commented to the woman clerk about her handwriting. The quality of that moment was changed. The woman felt appreciated and became more pleasant.

During your day, if you find a person or two who will not give you a smile, why not give them one of yours? It won't cost you a cent and takes little energy, but oh, what power of goodness it can generate.

"Never lose an opportunity of seeing anything that is beautiful," said Ralph Waldo Emerson. "Beauty is God's handwriting...a wayside sacrament. Welcome it in every fair face, in every fair sky, in every fair flower, and thank God for it as a cup of blessing."

A married couple serving as companions in Philippines had to take their daily showers in a basic facility with an uncertain water supply. It was not like their luxurious tile bath at home, free of crawling creatures and laden with lush towels. But they didn't complain to the natives! The woman reminded herself that as a child her favorite hot summer day activity was to run through lawn sprinklers and squish worms on the sidewalk with her bare feet. Each time she said this to her companion it turned feelings of complaint into laughter — changing the moment every time.

When they returned home, their stories of the daily shower challenge triggered the essence of their mission experience: "Wonderful — anyway!"

John Wesley had a mission of his own that had an impact on many lives during the last two hundred years. "Do all the good you can, by all the means you can, at all the times you can, in all the places you can, to all the people you can, as long as ever you can," he wrote. Lines to memorize and repeat, to think about and live by. Perfect counsel for a missionary.

St. Francis of Assisi lived in the twelfth century and did an enormous amount of good in his corner of the early Christian world. His philosophy of life has been put to music.

It has changed lives for the better and surely affected the quality of many a day by moving people to look at all moments in life as having valuable possibilities:

Lord,

make me an instrument of Your

peace.

Where there is hatred let me sow

love;

Where there is injury, pardon;

Where there is doubt, faith;

Where there is despair, hope;

Where there is darkness, light; and

Where there is sadness, joy.

O Divine Master,

grant that I may not so much

Seek to be consoled as to console,

To be understood as to understand;

To be loved as to love;

For it is in giving that we receive;

It is in pardoning that we are pardoned; and

It is in dying that we are born to

eternal life.

Jesus was our example in all things. Here are some golden moments that a missionary might relate to. He said:

Whosoever shall smite thee on thy right cheek, turn to

him the other also (Matthew 5:39).

If any man will sue thee at the law, and take away thy coat, let him have thy cloke also (Matthew 5:40).

Whosoever shall compel thee to go a mile, go with him twain (Matthew 5:41).

Love your enemies, bless them that curse you, do good to them that hate you (Matthew 5:44).

Leave there thy gift before the altar, and go thy way; first be reconciled to thy brother, and then come and offer thy gift (Matthew 7:12).

Forgive men their trespasses (Matthew 6:14).

Whosoever shall give to drink one of these little ones a cup of cold water only,...he shall in no wise lose his reward (Matthew 10:42).

I then, your Lord and Master, have washed your feet, ye also ought to wash one another's feet.

For, I have given you an example...

the servant is not greater than his lord; neither he that is sent greater than he that sent him.

If ye know these things, happy are ye if ye do them (John 13:14-17).

As you try to live more closely to the Jesus' teachings, as you try to make life more pleasant for others, as you conscientiously try to find those who will listen to the truth, as you look for beauty and goodness about you wherever you are and whatever kind of climate or circumstance you labor under, you will find moments to make golden by your action and attitude and caring.

You can change the quality of a day or a life.

Why not record these golden moments in your journal? Remember, a life recorded is a life twice lived.

15

BAPTISM, THE PURPOSE
OF MISSIONARY WORK

As you prepare for your mission, consider seriously the importance of baptism. This is really the purpose of missionary work — to bring people to Christ, to show them the way back to Heavenly Father's presence. What Mormons believe about baptism is quite different from what other churches believe.

We believe that it must be done by those having proper authority from God and by immersion. Baptize comes from the Greek *baptizo* meaning "immerse." Sprinkling doesn't do it!

We believe it is accepting Jesus as the Christ.

We believe that baptism is for the remission of sins, for covenants with Christ, for taking upon us the name and work of the Savior, for being born again, for preparing to receive the Holy Ghost. Baptism as we know it in The Church of Jesus Christ is necessary to enter the celestial kingdom.

Because of the Lord's goodness and personal sacrifice, all men will be saved — that is, resurrected. But unless a person is born of water and the Spirit and is pure, he cannot be exalted. Baptism opens the way for all other saving and exalting ordinances prescribed by God for man's growth and fitness for the Celestial kingdom.

Joseph Smith said, "Every man lives for himself. Adam

was made to open the way of the world, and for dressing the garden. Noah was born to save seed of everything, when the earth was washed of its wickedness by the flood; and the Son of God came into the world to redeem it from the fall. But except a man be born again, he cannot see the kingdom of God. This eternal truth settles the question of all men's religion. A man may be saved, after the judgment, in the terrestrial kingdom, or in the telestial kingdom, but he can never see the celestial kingdom of God, without being born of water and the Spirit. He may receive a glory like unto the moon, [I.e. of which the light of the moon is typical], or a star, [i. e. of which the light of the star is typical], but he can never come unto Mount Zion, and unto the city of the living God, the heavenly Jerusalem, and to an innumerable company of angels" *(Teachings of The Prophet Joseph Smith,* comp. by Joseph Fielding Smith; [Salt Lake City: Deseret Book Co., 1938], p. 12).

There is also something else for the missionary to remember. Jesus preached baptism to his disciples both in the Holy Land and during his ministry on the ancient American continent.

To the disciples in Jerusalem, Jesus said, "Go ye therefore, and teach all nations, baptizing them in the name of the Father, and of the Son, and of the Holy Ghost: teaching them to observe all things whatsoever I have commanded you: and, lo, I am with you alway, even unto the end of the world. Amen" (Matthew 28:19,20).

Jesus went on to say that of those baptized, he who believes shall be saved, and "he that believeth not shall be damned" (Mark 16:16). Surely there is no more explicit way of describing the importance of proper baptism!

Believers will be known from the unbelievers because true believers will be followed by spiritual gifts, such as healing by laying hands on the sick.

Christ's appearance to the people of Nephi began with his introduction by Heavenly Father himself. This is recorded in 3 Nephi 11. It is a thrilling chapter. In his first teachings to these people, the Savior emphasized baptism again and again. In this one chapter alone, the word *baptism* is mentioned thirteen times! It is in this Book of Mormon account that we learn from the Savior exactly how baptism should be done.

Little children who are not yet accountable, who have not reached eight years of age, do not need to be baptized.

In The Church of Jesus Christ of Latter-day Saints, we know that baptism is completed only when the gift of the Holy Ghost is conferred. It is required that we be immersed in water and then confirmed as members of the Church to receive the gift of the Holy Ghost. Latter-day Saints should be reminded to say, "When are you going to be baptized and confirmed?" One ordinance is not complete without the other.

Adam was baptized and confirmed. When the Lord had taught Adam, Adam cried unto the Lord and then was carried away by the Spirit of the Lord, brought down into the water; and immersed fully before being brought forth out of the water. "Thus he was baptized, and the Spirit of God descended upon him, and thus he was born of the Spirit, and became quickened in the inner man" (Moses 6:64:65).

Jesus was baptized and confirmed. The scriptures imply that Jesus walked down into the River Jordan with John the Baptist, who placed him under the water in baptism. "And Jesus, when he was baptized, went up straightway out of the water: and, lo, the heavens were opened unto him, and he saw the Spirit of God descending like a dove, and lighting upon him: and lo a voice from heaven, saying, This is my beloved Son, in whom I am well pleased" (Matthew 3:16,17).

To a baptized Mormon, the ordinance performed through immersion and confirmation constitutes a covenant with God that we have taken upon us the Savior's name and work and that we will remember that he died for us, was buried in the tomb, and came forth resurrected. Each time he or she takes the sacrament, the newly baptized person will be reminded of these covenants. The bread reminds us of Christ's flesh and the water represents his blood. The sacramental prayers are for us to listen to carefully; we respond with an "Amen" that we agree that we will always remember him and keep the commandments which he has given us so that we may always have his Spirit to be with us.

In return, the Savior promises to forgive us our sins and to give us eternal life with him and Heavenly Father when we have finished our time on earth.

Wonderful! How totally wonderful!

16

THE KEY TO
CONVERSION

The Book of Mormon is the key to conversion. We ourselves can — and must — become truly converted to the gospel we share with others. Many investigators recognize the truth of the work and the divinity of Christ as they read the Book of Mormon.

The Lord expects us to use the Book of Mormon in proselyting activity — not only to learn what is contained in the book itself, but also to learn how to effectively use it with every contact we make in missionary work.

President Ezra Taft Benson has said that the Book of Mormon needs to become more central in our preaching, our teaching, and our missionary work: "We must flood the earth with the Book of Mormon.... I have a vision of homes alerted, of classes alive, and of pulpits aflame with the spirit of Book of Mormon messages.... I have a vision of the whole Church getting nearer to God by abiding by the precepts of the Book of Mormon." (*Ensign,* November 1988, pp. 5, 6.)

This is a prophet of God speaking.

The missionary who uses the Book of Mormon for personal preparation and as a standard for life and who also makes it the center of teaching and personal study will see great strides made in the work of bringing people to Christ.

Most of us need to repent in this matter.

President Marion G. Romney said, "The Book of Mormon is the most effective piece of missionary literature we have" (*Improvement Era,* June 1960, p. 435).

The Prophet Joseph Smith said that the Book of Mormon is the keystone of our religion, and that reading it will bring us closer to the Lord than any other book on earth.

When we ourselves or someone to whom we are teaching the gospel accepts the Book of Mormon as true, consider what happens:

1. If we accept the Book of Mormon, we accept Joseph Smith as a prophet of God.

2. If Joseph Smith was a prophet of God, the First Vision was a reality.

3. If the First Vision was a reality, the priesthood was in fact restored to the earth.

4. If the priesthood of God was restored through angels under the direction of God, the Doctrine and Covenants, Pearl of Great Price, and other LDS scriptures are valid.

5. If the priesthood and the accompanying ordinances were restored, the organization of The Church of Jesus Christ of Latter-day Saints is the institution of God restored on earth today — in fact, not only name.

6. If Christ's church is restored, it is led by his prophets, to whom he continues to reveal his mind and will, his purposes for his children on earth, and the direction his church should go to accomplish those purposes.

7. Through the Church we become aware of our eternal heritage and of eternal relationships and future possibilities.

8. All of these things strengthen our witness that Jesus is the Christ and that there is purpose to the Creation, to his ministry, to all the unfolding of truth, and to all eternity.

The Book of Mormon stands as another witness to Christ. It shows the great things that God has done for people in the past. It makes us aware of the promises for people in the future. It shows the continuity of truth that God's children in every age and time need to make it back to his presence.

The Book of Mormon is true. It will bring people to Christ. Conversion is the basis of your call to serve a mission.

You want people to become converted to Christ, not to a book, however grand, nor to yourself, however good, loving, caring, and charming! If people are converted to Christ and not to you, they are more likely to stay strong in the faith even if you move on to other assignments and other places.

The Book of Mormon is true. It is also valuable. It reveals to readers the precious example of Jesus Christ. The stirring witness of Christ that comes with a sincere reading of the Book of Mormon is almost overwhelming. Doctrine is detailed within its pages that has come directly from Christ as he taught the ancient Americans; that has come from Christ's special servants, called by him as you have been; and that has been revealed to those servants through the power of the Holy Ghost for the good of mankind. If we follow these truths, we will find our way back home to heaven — to live, after judgment day, in the presence of God the Father.

Among other things, the Book of Mormon teaches people how to pray, whom to pray to, what to pray for, and what to expect following prayer.

It teaches what to do about how you feel in a spiritual experience and how to draw on the powers of heaven.

It teaches about the Holy Ghost, how the Holy Ghost works in an individual, and how the Holy Ghost is lost.

It delineates the ramifications of guilt — what happens to the Spirit when a person suffers from sin and how repentance is brought about, with incredible examples of those who have repented and found peace before God.

It teaches the value of obedience: children and parents,

prophets and God; the blessing of obeying principles irrevocably decreed in heaven before this world was; the importance of personally obeying God's will for the unique individual; an understanding of the fruits of obedience, the freedom and fulfillment of God's will, and the joy in receiving his rewards.

It teaches of inspired ordinances, of effective government and financial systems, of spiritual gifts, of yardsticks to know right from wrong, and of the miracle of revelation. It teaches of the awesome love God has for each one and of his particular joy with those who do his will. It teaches of the peril of sin and of the joy in faithful living, patience, love, and service; of strength in stewardship; and of power in purity.

We believe the Bible to be a witness of Jesus Christ and true as far as it is translated correctly. But we in The Church of Jesus Christ of Latter-day Saints testify that the Book of Mormon is the most perfectly translated book on earth because it was done through the power of the Holy Ghost under the direction of God.

The Book of Mormon is another witness of Christ. We witness that it is true!

Anyone can know the Book of Mormon is true. If you read this book and ask God "with a sincere heart, with real intent, having faith in Christ, he will manifest the truth of it unto you, by the power of the Holy Ghost. And by the power of the Holy Ghost ye may know the truth of all things." (Moron) 10:4-5.)

17

The Songs of the Righteous

Every missionary will want to become familiar with hymns of praise, hymns of joy, hymns that motivate individuals to the work of the Lord, hymns that remind of sacred gospel principles and tender relationships.

The Lord commanded Emma, wife of the Prophet Joseph Smith, to make a selection of sacred hymns, as it would be given to her, that would be pleasing to Him. He said, "For my soul delighteth in the song of the heart; yea, the song of the righteous is a prayer unto me, and it shall be answered with a blessing upon their heads" (D&C 25:12).

Take time for the time it takes to turn an ordinary gathering of whatever size into a significant experience by introducing a hymn. Hymns change the moment, brighten the event, lift the mood, light the way, mark the day, make any gathering better, and do great good.

Here are some of the beloved LDS hymns that a missionary can especially benefit from. Memorize the inspired words. Internalize the message. Look and listen to the hymns in a new way, remembering that the songs of the righteous delight the heart of the Lord. They contain sermons for a variety of formal occasions.

75

CALLED TO SERVE

Called to serve Him, heav'nly King of glory,
Chosen e'er to witness for his name,
Far and wide we tell the Father's story,
Far and wide his love proclaim.
Onward, ever onward, as we glory in his name;
Onward, ever onward, as we glory in his name;
Forward, pressing forward, as a triumph song we sing.
God our strength will be; press forward ever,
Called to serve our King.

(Text: Grace Gordon; music: Walter G. Tyler. *Hymns* [1985], no. 249.)

TEACH ME TO WALK IN THE LIGHT

Teach me to walk in the light of his love;
Teach me to pray to my Father above;
Teach me to know of the things that are right;
Teach me, teach me to walk in the light.

(Text and music: Clara W. McMaster. *Hymns* [1985], no. 304.)

MORE HOLINESS GIVE ME

More holiness give me,
More strivings within,
More patience in suff'ring,
More sorrow for sin,
More faith in my Savior,
More sense of his care,
More joy in his service,
More purpose in prayer.

More gratitude give me,
More trust in the Lord,
More pride in his glory,
More hope in his word,
More tears for his sorrows,

More pain at his grief,
More meekness in trial,
More praise for relief.

More purity give me,
More strength to o'ercome,
More freedom from earthstains,
More longing for home.
More fit for the kingdom,
More used would I be,
More blessed and holy,
More, Savior, like thee.

(Text and music: Philip Paul Bliss. *Hymns* [1985], no. 131.)

LOVE ONE ANOTHER

As I have loved you,
Love one another.
This new commandment:
Love one another.
By this shall men know
Ye are my disciples,
If ye have love
One to another.

(Text and music: Luacine Clark Fox. *Hymns* [1985], no. 308.)

I BELIEVE IN CHRIST

I believe in Christ; he is my King!
With all my heart to him I'll sing;
I'll raise my voice in praise and joy,
In grand amens my tongue employ.
I believe in Christ; he is God's Son.
On earth to dwell his soul did come.
He healed the sick; the dead he raised.
Good works were his; his name be praised.

(Text: Bruce R. McConkie music: John Longhurst. *Hymns* [1985], no. 134. "I Believe in Christ" © The Church of Jesus Christ of Latter-day Saints. Used by permission.)

I NEED THEE EVERY HOUR

I need thee every hour,
Most gracious Lord.
No tender voice like shine
Can peace afford.

I need thee, oh, I need thee;
Every hour I need thee!
Oh, bless me now, my Savior;
I come to thee!

I need thee every hour;
Stay thou nearby.
Temptations lose their pow'r
When thou art nigh.

I need thee every hour,
In joy or pain.
Come quickly and abide,
Or life is vain.

I need thee every hour,
Most holy One.
Oh, make me thine indeed,
Thou blessed Son!

(Text: Annie S. Hawkes; music: Robert Lowry. *Hymns,* no. 98.)

LET US ALL PRESS ON

Let us all press on in the work of the Lord,
That when life is o'er we may gain a reward;
In the fight for right let us wield a sword,

The mighty sword of truth.

We will not retreat, though our numbers may be few
When compared with the opposite host in view;
But an unseen pow'r will aid me and you
In the glorious cause of truth.

If we do what's right we have no need to fear,
For the Lord, our helper, will ever be near;
In the days of trial his Saints he will cheer,
And prosper the cause of truth.

Fear not, though the enemy deride;
Courage, for the Lord is on our side.
We will heed not what the wicked may say,
But the Lord alone we will obey.

(Text and music: Evan Stephens. *Hymns,* no. 243.)

Now that you know the words, sing them with enthusiasm!

18

Do the Right Things
in the Right Way

In missionary work as well as life, we are continually bombarded with things to do in order to survive, as well as to have some pleasure in living and achieving.

In school, business, and church service, we are asked to give reports. Sometimes they are verbal and sometimes written. Sometimes these reports describe what we did with words and sometimes with numbers. Our Heavenly Father requires an accounting of our stewardship. We must constantly be alert to ensure that our personal growth relates to past performance and that we are improving in our efforts.

To be a success, a person needs vision and a plan for accomplishment. When following the plan, applying eternal principles to reach the goal makes the difference in how people achieve their goal. Doing the right things in the right way and for the right reasons increases the missionary's capacity to show the pure love of Christ, to be an example of the true disciple.

There is an old legend about the building of a great cathedral. The brick masons working on the building had different answers as to what they were doing. One was earning his livelihood. One was building a wall. One was building a cathedral unto the Lord. Each was doing essentially the same task, but each viewed it differently. Their perception was determined by their vision and attitude. The mason can keep his mind on the ultimate goal — a beautiful cathedral.

Likewise, missionaries should always remember that the work they are called to do is inspired, whether it is filling mundane reports or planning and planning again a week's activities. This is a large part of achieving the dreamed-of success.

A mother, as she works in the house doing unlimited tasks, can keep in mind her purpose of having a celestial home, of rearing a family unto the Lord.

The dentist, daily doing the same work over and over — drilling and filling, drilling and filling — can remember that he is helping someone be free of pain!

The missionary will be blessed who comes to realize that the planning work is the spiritual creation of any accomplishment. The regular reporting work is accounting for one's stewardship and is essential to fulfill the measure of one's creation as an individual or as a missionary. Your ability to work under the influence of the Spirit to find and baptize God's prepared children on earth — this success rises as plans are made, goals are set, effort is put forth, and an account is given by way of report through prayer to the Lord and formal reports to the mission president. Learning to report is vital to one's eternal progress.

Sometimes missionaries become "pushers of the program" and worry about the number of discussions they give rather than viewing themselves as servants of their fellowmen. Missionaries can become immersed in the doing of things rather than in the blessing of lives. Certain things need to be done, but to do these things right — right away, in the right way—is in line with the sacred but practical aspects of missionary work.

Take a moment daily to look in the mirror. Remember your purpose in being on a mission. Remember that you have come a long way, but you still have a long way to become "as He is." Look in the mirror, then turn away to thrust in your sickle with all your heart, might, mind, and strength. Then one day you can stand blameless before the Lord and reap the blessings—joy, peace, eternal life—that come from doing the right things in the right way.

19

WINNING HEARTS TO
CHANGE LIVES

In about 74 B.C. in ancient America, Alma headed a mission to reclaim some of their friends and loved ones who had left the main church and had become apostates. They were so far removed from the traditions of their fathers that they had built a tower which they called Rameumptom. Each person would climb this tower, one at a time, and stretch forth his hands toward heaven and give thanks that it had been "made known" to him that there "shall be no Christ." It was an incredible shock to Alma and those he had taken with him on this special mission.

Alma took Ammon, Aaron, Omner, Zeezrom, Amulek, and two of his sons, named Shiblon and Corianton. Alma knew that the word of God had a more powerful effect upon the minds and hearts of the people than the sword, or anything else. So Alma decided to try the virtue of the word of God with the Zoramite people, as they were called. He did everything right for the mission. His cause was a good one. He chose fine men as companions. He prayed earnestly to the Lord for success in the work and that they would be comforted, strengthened, and able to bear affliction which might come upon them because of the wickedness of the people. Then he "clapped his hands upon all who were with him...and they were filled with the Holy Ghost." (See Alma 31:1-36.)

The work didn't go forward as successfully as they had hoped, but their compassion won the hearts of some. Alma's team was willing to teach the poor people who had been banned from the synagogues because their clothing wasn't good enough. They won their hearts, changed their lives, and imparted some of their lands for an inheritance to them when they returned home to Zarahemla (see Alma 35:14).

Ammon's missionary approach when he was teaching the Lamanites is one for missionaries to study repeatedly. He served their king, Lamoni, before he taught him or his people (see Alma 17:29). He did not mention the reason for his mission or teach any gospel principles at the beginning of his service to the king.

By his incredible example of service, he prepared them to be ready to receive the gospel.

It has been said many times by many teachers and leaders: people do not care how much you know until they know how much you care. Ammon acted according to that truth.

Ammon's intent was "to win the hearts" of the Lamanites through service. In doing so, he was able to influence them and touch their hearts sufficiently so that many were converted. (see Alma 17-19).

Later, Ammon and King Lamoni met Lamoni's father, who commanded Lamoni to slay Ammon. But Lamoni would not. Then the father sought to do so himself. However, Ammon prevailed against him and could have slain the man, but he chose to spare his life.

Lamoni's father was impressed by Ammon's great love for his son, the king. Because of this incident and Ammon's example of fairness and compassion, Aaron was later able to teach the father of King Lamoni. He, too, began his gospel teaching by offering to serve the older man (see Alma 20, 22).

Each of us has talents, abilities, hobbies, and experiences that can be used to win people's hearts, similar to the experience of Ammon and Aaron. We may use them to serve others in love and to prepare them to be receptive to the gospel.

President Kimball declared missionary work to be very effective when missionaries work together with members. Missionaries can serve the leaders of a branch, the quorum president or Relief Society president, and others. Through offering this help the missionaries gain the support of the leaders so that members are willing to share the gospel with their nonmember friends.

Such service to local members can be anything that shows love and caring, from cleaning the church to preparing cookies for a fireside. With such an aura of caring for each other, soon members open their homes to investigators. This is one of the best ways to win the hearts of those you want to teach the gospel to.

We prepare our own hearts to win other hearts by applying this scripture: "Who shall ascend into the hill of the Lord? or who shall stand in his holy place? He that hath clean hands, and a pure heart" (Psalm 24:3-4). When we are pure, the Holy Ghost can work through us to benefit others with the fulness of the gospel. Then lives change.

20

LOVE

Many a new missionary has gone forth to share the gospel so full of good spirit, so profoundly touched with new-found love for the Lord, that when the first door opens at his knock, something wonderful happens. The individual hears the missionary's plea, "Oh, won't you please listen?" He notices the missionary's tears and senses the accompanying emotions of earnestness, nervousness, and love. Then he says, "Oh, come on in...."

Love breaks down every barrier.

Matthew Cowley, a great man of faith and love, has been credited with saying, "Live to learn, learn to love, and you'll love to live." You'll find that when you feel loved, you feel good. If you give love, you feel good. If you share love, you will feel close to the Lord Jesus Christ.

Jesus made the subject of love a test of those who were his disciples. He said that according to how they loved one another "shall all men know that ye are my disciples" (John 3:35). Every missionary — every person — should yearn and live to become a true disciple of Christ. Such a goal is the very essence of life.

Jesus taught the importance of love. We learn that love can be far reaching, and be the center not only of every person's life, but also of every Church program's purpose and of every principle to bring people to exaltation.

Jesus said we should love even those who are not our favorite people, who might have done us a disservice, treated us poorly or rudely, who might be said to be our enemies. He took mankind a step higher in ideal behavior. (See Matthew 5:43-48.)

Jesus said that if we only have love for those who love us, we are remiss. He pointed out that even sinners love those who love them. But, said Jesus, "Love ye your enemies, and do good, and lend, hoping for nothing again; and your reward shall be great, and ye shall be the children of the Highest: for he is kind unto the unthankful and to the evil." (Luke 6:32-35.)

We should keep this goal ever in mind as we respond to a call to serve. To become like Jesus is to become children of the Highest. How much more suited we'll be as his children to bring other people to the truth of the gospel and the way of life that guides people back into the presence of the Highest!

Jesus warmed our hearts concerning how we should treat each other, what we should feel for each other, and what we should demonstrate through daily acts of caring one for another.

Jesus used the tender example of the lost sheep mourned by its shepherd. Jesus is the Great Shepherd and we are his helpers. We are to feed his sheep; we are to find the lost sheep. We are to rescue people from the ways of the world. We are to feed them the gospel and thus infuse them with ideals and goals to strive for. We are to inspire them by sharing the gospel truths and witnessing that Jesus Christ is the Savior, the Son of God.

Jesus was amazing — we stand amazed at the love he offered each of us. Consider his forgiveness for the woman taken in sin; his patience with Martha, who was cumbered with much serving; his example as a leader and master in humbly washing the feet of his disciples!

It was a cultural courtesy of the times to offer the first taste of the banquet to someone who was esteemed as a valued friend. This "sop," as the scriptures called the morsel — this honored first taste was what Christ offered to Judas. Knowing all the while that Judas was to be His betrayer, nonetheless, Christ honored and loved him. *And we who are called to serve the Savior are to be like him in loving!*

Jesus gave us the commandments which He called the greatest of all commandments: we should love God and we should love each other (see Matthew 22:36-40). He said, "Love one another, as I have loved you" (John 15:12). The depth of this love is more understandable when we think of Christ's example. Because Jesus loved us he endured —

- Incredible suffering by taking upon himself all the sins of mankind.
- Submitting to capture through the help of one of his chosen twelve Apostles.
- Obediently dying by crucifixion.

His love was so profound that when He was on the cross and suffering the most acute pain, He said, "Father, forgive them; for they know not what they do" (Luke 23:34).

Jesus was the exquisite initiator of the principle of enduring love and personal sacrifice. He said, "Greater love hath no man than this, that a man lay down his life for his friends. Ye are my friends" (John 15:13-14).

Jesus was the superb — as well as the supreme example of love. We look to him as the ideal for living in happiness as families, as Latter-day Saints, as co-workers, and as associates in our verious communities.

Jesus taught us ultimate love when He said, "If a man love me, he will keep my words: and my Father will love him, and we will come unto him, and make our abode with him" (John 14:23).

This commandment is easy to keep — providing individuals will polish and hone, modifying their feelings and behaviors, doing as Christ would do, feeling as Christ would feel about others. This kind of love is indeed an awesome understanding for us to arrive at. No longer do we behave by duty, rote, and obedience to a set of laws; rather, we love for the peace it brings, the joy and the heaven on earth.

The world largely has failed and forgotten this love. We must not.

What is there in life if not to make things more pleasant for each other? The Savior's commandments and examples of love encourage this possibility. A kind of heaven on earth can become a reality, at least in private corners where Christlike love is practiced.

People not only survive, they also thrive more readily in an atmosphere of love. They can better endure sorrow, stress, striving, and life crises when they feel supported and pleasantly accepted by loving friends and family.

In a world where people help people professionally, how good it is when compassion accompanies the doctor's diagnosis, the auto mechanic's labor, or the services of cleaning help and waitresses.

Jesus said, "Let thy love abound unto all men, and unto all who love my name" (D&C 112:11).

This is not the easiest principle heaven has given us to live, but it is the most rewarding when put into action. We hark back to the night when Jesus was born and the angels said, "On earth peace, good will toward men." It marked the beginning of a new emotional understanding of life's possibilities. For everyone called to serve, this anthem is a new beginning for hope in human relationships.

21

THAT YOU MAY BE
FILLED

Thinking about the thinking of great thinkers often provides a new perspective for your own point of view. When you are called to serve the Lord, you share the gospel with someone who wants to grow in understanding and application of eternal principles. This is a mighty responsibility. You may be the only link, at the moment, between the Church and that individual. You may be the only opportunity or source of information and example to someone thus far deprived of the freeing, saving, exhilarating truth found in the restored gospel.

Thomas Hardy said:

> Passion is a bad counselor.
>
> Quit vicious habits.
>
> Encourage diligence.
>
> Forget not past favours.

Thomas Hardy was right. His lines are based on God's eternal truth. Passions misused can lead you carefully away from the fold of the Good Shepherd and into chains of darkness and misery.

The Lord spoke through the prophet Alma to all of us when he said, "See that ye bridle all your passions, that ye may be filled with love" (Alma 38:12).

Love is that grand emotion — love of God and love of others brings value of self as a literal child of God. Remember always that the Spirit of God cannot dwell in any unclean thing. Destructive passions are "unclean" and prohibit God's love from flooding your soul and influencing your motives and actions.

What passions destroy love?

What passions need to be bridled or controlled so that holy affection, compassion, respect, and regard for the worth of the souls of the children of God will grow within our hearts and minds?

What protection must be given to the soul of each person so that the Lord's influences and sweet emotions may fill our beings?

Consuming emotions that give us little space for thoughts of love or anything else include hate, anger, jealousy, greed, lust, selfishness, idleness, procrastination, vengeance, self-righteousness, doubt, guilt, fear, conceit, pride, and self-pity. Think about it. When you are angry at someone, you don't feel like running up and throwing your arms around her in warm affection! When a person has wronged you unjustly, it takes mighty, fervent prayer to control your feelings of anger and to subdue plans for revenge. Prayer for help to behave — such as Christ has taught and still teaches today through his prophets — such prayer can be life-changing. To live with any un-Christlike attitude surging through your being is to put your toe on the devil's turf.

When you are called to serve, you can teach and share Christ's precepts effectively *only if your toe is not on the devil's turf.* Love and hate do not walk the same path. Love cannot fill the heart to generate life's actions if hate is stirring up a storm inviting the forces of foolishness and evil.

To strengthen your understanding, study afresh the Ten Commandments; the Beatitudes; the Articles of Faith; the sacrament prayers; and the covenants we make with the Lord in baptism and confirmation in accepting priesthood ordinations and calls to serve in Church capacities, and in temple ordinances. Feast upon the word of the Lord in the scriptures. Listen to the brethren and sisters in leadership positions for inspiration to strengthen your resolve to bridle your passions.

"And now, as ye have begun to teach the word even so I would that ye should continue to teach; and I would that ye would be diligent and temperate in all things. See that you are not lifted up unto pride; yea, see that ye do not boast in your own wisdom, nor of your much strength.... See that you refrain from idleness.... Do not say: O God, I thank thee that we are better than our brethren; but rather say: O Lord, forgive my unworthiness, and remember my brethren in mercy — yea, acknowledge your unworthiness before God at all times" (Alma 38:10-12, 14.)

Then get worthy!

Pythagoras said, "Know this for truth, and learn to conquer these: thy belly first; sloth, luxury, and rage. Do nothing base with others or alone. And, above all, thine own self, respect."

Begin developing positive relationships with others. Pick a day and choose a person. Then say something kind, helping, supportive, and true! Everyone needs approval; everyone loves to be loved.

You can say things like this:

- You are a blessing to this mission (or your family, zone, to our generation, to the Lord's work)!
- You really know and understand the scriptures!
- I like myself better when I am with you. What a great influence you are!

- You take the corners smoothly, Brother.
- You are really one believable Elder.
- You were born to win, no matter what.

There is such comfort in that portion of the scripture that deals with the reward of bridling all one's passions. Because thoughts precede actions, understand that when you bridle your passions so that you may be filled with love, how satisfying life and relationships can be!

22

Make a Note of It

Some people believe that a well-tied tie is the first serious step in a young man's life. Others say it is the day you land your first job. The truth of the matter of things that matter is that learning to keep records of the important things really is the Big Day of all the rest of your life.

Make a note of it. Watch it come true.

Keep a calendar of your events, including a list of birthdays of people you love, medical appointments, promises to keep, Church assignments, appointments to teach the gospel, and good ideas that come to you in the night. Check your schedule, and do not procrastinate the timing of what you are supposed to do.

As David said to Solomon when he gave him instructions regarding the building of the temple, "Be strong and of good courage, and do it" (1 Chronicles 28:20). Get organized and you'll do it when it is supposed to be done. Then you'll do much good in the kingdom.

The Lord takes a serious view of records. He spoke to all of us with these words: "Write the things which ye have seen and heard, save it be those which are forbidden.... For behold, out of the books which have been written, and which shall be written, shall this people be judged, for by them shall their works be known unto men. And behold, all things are written by the Father; therefore out of the books which shall be written shall the world be judged." (3 Nephi 27:23, 25-26.)

That's the truth — you will be judged by the records you keep, by your own book of acts. If there is no record . . . ! Do you recall how seriously the Lord takes record keeping? When he visited the Nephite people in ancient America, He told them to bring forth the records they had kept. Then He chastised them for not recording a certain prophecy about His own coming. Here He was in person, the prophecy fulfilled, yet He insisted on the prophecy being included in the records. (See 3 Nephi 23:613.)

When you are anxiously engaged in a good cause, you are busy. You need a mighty list, a record book, and a habit of taking notes of what you learn and feel, of inspiring ideas and spiritual promptings, of insights about the scriptures and tasks you need to do, of people you must thank, of items to record in your personal journal, or of an official record you might be called to keep for the mission, the branch, or the company.

Keep track of what you learn, what you feel, what you do, whom you meet. Especially make a record of your relationship with God — prayers answered, blessings bestowed, forgiveness given, inspiration felt, ordinances participated in, witnesses of the Spirit. You'll benefit by making a note of conversations that have moved you, lessons you have learned, temptations you have overcome, and struggles you have suffered but survived spiritually intact.

If you don't write it, you'll forget it.

When you are reading the scriptures, marginal notes help you recall something that impresses you or a special understanding that you have received about that scripture or gospel principle.

A note written is an idea retained.

Joseph Smith bought himself a personal record book soon after he received the revelation that the Church should keep records. Inside the front cover he wrote that he had bought the book to keep a record of all the things that came under his observation. That is a good idea!

A life recorded is a life twice-lived. You'll learn from your notes; you'll recall precious times by your notes. You'll be obeying commandments if you do make a note of things you are inspired to write about. Let the Spirit be your guide. But be sure you are in tune with the Spirit and don't miss a note you ought to be making.

Write so you'll remember! Do it!

23

STAY TOGETHER

O ne of the strongest counsels given to departing missionaries is "Stay together!" This applies to the young Elders,
to the Sister missionaries, and to couples. The command to
stay together is given for a good reason — the protection of
the missionary and the production of the work.

The gospel is spread in pairs. Missionary work is accomplished two by two. When one is weak, the other can stand
as a strong reminder to —

- Be positive.
- Be obedient.
- Keep striving.
- Hang in there. Study the scriptures. Keep mission rules
  faithfully. Adhere to the mission schedule of study,
  prayer, rest, and meditation.
- Guard against succumbing to temptation.
- Help each other find suitable ways to get recreation.
- Consider ways to find investigators.
- Pray together, fast together, study together, do good
  deeds together, support each other.
- Encourage each other to write home regularly.
- Think of mission and not yearn over loved ones at
  home and their problems.

Remember the good rule: Stay Together. You are your companion's keeper. As you care for each other, you can come to love each other. You will get along better in such a close relationship. Stay Together means that if your companion leaves to get a drink, you get a drink. If your companion goes to the restroom, you go and stand outside the restroom.

Stay Together is a safe and sound slogan, strongly made. There are countless horror stories — sad but true tales — of mission field tragedies that occur when companions do not stay together. After trouble comes, someone might say by way of excuse, "Oh, they were only gone a minute." In what may have seemed like a minute, Satan was at work and virtue was lost! Or some other kind of crisis occurred. Dishonorable release is the next step.

You are a special servant called to serve the Lord Jesus Christ. We all know that there is a spiritual war on for the souls of men. Satan is dedicated to thwart your mission. Obedience to God's commands and to the protective and productive guidelines established for missionaries by the Church authorities is the way to overcome the adversary!

Help each be what a missionary should be. Love each other as a disciple of Christ, that encouragement for each other will be readily given and easily accepted. Pray together — set a schedule, plead your case before God. Remind each other of the importance of praying together as well as having personal, private prayer. However, confessing to each other that you pray for each other in personal, private prayer can be strengthening. Kneeling in prayer together as companions in the service of God — like Peter and James, Alma and Amulek,, Joseph and Hyrum, the sons of Mosiah — allows the Holy Spirit to descend upon you both. A blessed bonding can happen.

So stay together. Pray together. Watch over each other, together in sickness, in service, in yearning for home, in confusion about the work. You are missionaries for the Lord Jesus Christ, and that makes all the difference. Your call to serve, and your assignment to serve with each other at a given time are under the inspiration of the Lord.

24

CREATION, ORGANIZATION, AND TIME

You are a creator You are in the process of creating many things in your life, but the greatest creation you will ever work with will be yourself and your fellowmen.

The meaning of *create* is not to construct out of nothing, but to organize, to put in order, to give form, to put in working condition. The purpose of God's work of creation is to bring about "the immortality and eternal life of man" (Moses 1:39), to bring mankind to its highest potential.

How is your work of creation going? Are you progressing towards eternal life and helping others to do the same? After all, that is why we are here on earth — to create and, in a future setting, to become eternal creators. The work of creation — of order, organization, and improvement — is eternal. We will never create great character or assist others until we learn to organize ourselves! Organization is creation. To be an effective creator in our own life and in the lives of others, we must use all our available resources — especially our time, energies, and skills — by applying the principles of creation to put our resources to work in their proper place.

Time is one of our greatest resources in building a beautiful creation. We can make better use of our time by daily evaluating our situation, setting goals, planning, implementing the plans, adapting our plans to bless lives, and reevaluating

---

our performance. Organization brings greater success.

A plan of creation, made of inspired goals, can help us follow a more direct course in achieving our divinely appointed purposes. As we accept accountability for our goals, we will plead with the Lord for strength to achieve them and then apply our efforts with much greater diligence to accomplish them.

It has been said, "Hell is the regret of lost opportunities." Applying the principles of creation and organization can help us make effective use of every opportunity and every moment as we strive to prepare and organize mankind for eternity. Written plans can save us time and conserve mental energy by focusing our efforts on our goals. Planning a physically efficient course will also save us time, which we can use for other improvements.

Organizing our materials and resources so that we can become better and reach higher every day is creation in its truest and most eternal sense. As we apply the principle of creation, our creations — our lives and the lives of others — will become more and more beautiful and be more and more blessed, and the power of the Lord will truly be with us in our work.

The Lord's work is urgent, and our time is limited. Without organization, there is little chance of our efforts resulting in beautiful creation. The doctrine of creation is imperative in leadership, and essential for continued success. The doctrine is eternal — applying it was the first thing the Father and Jehovah did at the beginning of this earthly project. We are to be like them (see 3 Nephi 12:48). Let us fulfill our measure of creation. Let us prepare and organize every needful thing (see D&C 88:119). We can do it, but we must pay the price with companionship inventory and nightly planning. Without these vital steps, we have chosen chaos, not creation.

Let us diligently do the work of creation in our own lives so we may participate in God's work of creation through bringing the beauty of the gospel into others' lives.

25

BY THE SWEAT OF THE MISSIONARIES' BROWS

The Lord gave to Father Adam the commandment to work "by the sweat of [his] brow." The law of work is a blessing, and has been fundamental to the growth and achievement of man since the beginning. Indeed, work is the price of lasting success.

People often fail to appreciate success that comes without effort, and thus they have little or no staying power for continued success. The sacrifice and work that lead to achievement make motivation to success more lasting and also produce good feelings that contribute to self-esteem. When people do not work their hardest, or when they know that their success was really a matter of circumstance rather than planning and personal effort, they do not increase in self-respect and self-worth.

Fundamental to progress and associated with the law of work are the laws of harvest and sacrifice. These laws operate daily in the mission field. A missionary may give scores of discussions in order to achieve one baptism. A full teaching pool is necessary in order to baptize continually. Things don't just happen. There is a price, even in the harvest of baptisms.

The law of sacrifice applies particularly to personal righteousness. We must submit ourselves to the Lord. We must sacrifice our will for God's will. We must offer up a broken heart and a contrite spirit. We must become proficient, exactly obedient, and totally disciplined to our commitments. The sacrifice this requires then becomes a power in our lives.

Just as Christ sacrificed for us to save us, likewise we give up certain things or so-called pleasures in order to save ourselves and others. When we sacrifice, we put God's will first in our lives and in our hearts. We become receptive to the Spirit. Sacrifice changes us within.

The law of sacrifice is an imperial truth. Without it, we die; with it, we live. Blessings come as we apply true principles. As we come to Christ and to God through faith, love, obedience, and sacrifice, God's truth and light will fill our souls.

The law of the harvest is best applied by "working smart." Effort without planning and forethought can be as fruitless as no work at all. Planning precedes performance. Principles of effective work include a workable plan, a reasonable time frame, systematic evaluation, accounting and reporting, delegation, and involvement of others. In mortality we must put priorities on our efforts and our time. We must plan our methods to achieve our objectives. Prioritizing our life, projects, and time can bring us greater success and a satisfying feeling of accomplishment.

Often, instead of working harder and longer, we simply need to remove the resisting forces. Evaluating where we are and where we want to go next can help us determine what to do to clear the path. Be wary of taking the path of least resistance; shortcuts can short-circuit our values. When we are led by the Spirit, the method — as well as the what, why, and where — will be revealed as we study it out in our mind and apply correct principles.

To do effective work we need goals, commitment, tools, vision, desire, effort, and the Lord God leading the way. Work and sacrifice are the Lord's eternal verities for man's success. The reward is joy (see Alma 29:9-10). With God leading us, we cannot fail.

26

GOOD COMMUNICATION
IN RELATIONSHIPS

Our experiences in mortal probation seem to be very much connected with our effectiveness in communication. Communication with God is essential to our eternal life. Communication with our fellowmen is essential in building satisfying relationships. Even the message of the Restoration itself centers around communication between God and man. Missionaries are communicators of this vital message.

As communicators, we must remember that communication — the process of sharing information, feelings, interests, and mutual concerns in order to develop empathy and understanding — depends on establishing relationships of love, trust, and respect. Between God and man, these relationships are developed by sacrifice, obedience, and faith. Just as sin keeps us from eternal life, failure to communicate keeps us from enjoying the fellowship of both God (see Ether 2:14) and man. The consequences of poor communication are devastating: lack of understanding, deterioration of lives and relationships, failures of goals and plans, and growth of negative feelings.

The positive effects of good communication, however, are great. Through such communication, we bless each other with words of encouragement and testimony. Good communication is a sign and principle of love. It depends

---

upon our forgetting self-interest, personal ego, and the need to be right; it depends upon developing Christlike love. Christlike love will give us an honest desire to understand another person's perceptions, emotions, and real underlying message. We may check our understanding by making clarifying statements or asking questions. We should listen carefully and ask for feedback. Understanding may not bring agreement, but it will improve relationships. Also, blaming never solves a problem; often we ourselves need to change and repent. Seek first to understand, then to be understood.

When we are filled with divine love, we will be positive in our demeanor, attitude, and speech, and we will radiate the Spirit in both word and action. We will consider each person's level of faith, understanding, concerns, needs, and interests. We will establish the proper atmosphere by resolving concerns, expressing love and concern, praying for him or her, and praying for the presence of the Spirit. We will say things in the right way, in the right spirit, and take time to communicate our true intent. We will be candid and honest, yet sensitive to the needs of the situation and the individual. Our goal will be to leave the other person feeling better for having visited with us.

When difficulties arise, we will remain humble (without blaming others), focus on the problem, analyze the situation, and generate possible solutions, broadening the options instead of looking for a single solution. We can stay open to solutions by asking "why" or "why not" instead of taking an immovable position. We will treat solving the problem as a mutual concern, and look for mutual gain in the solution, involving others in the decision where appropriate. When we ourselves need help, we will entreat others with love, be grateful for assistance, and express our need in a way that will bring about empathy and a desire to help.

Finally, we need to communicate honestly with ourselves through meditation, pondering, and self-evaluation. Total honesty is important. We must recognize our divine potential as well as our need to make changes, including the "mighty change," by repenting with a broken heart and a contrite spirit (see Alma 5:14). If we will purify ourselves and exercise great faith, God will give us powerful language, as he gave to Enoch (see Moses 7:13), Nephi, and the brother of Jared (see Ether 12:24-25), and the power of the Spirit will carry our message unto the hearts of men (see 2 Nephi 33:1).

27

OPEN YOUR MOUTH!

The Lord said, "Open your mouths and they shall be filled, and you shall become even as Nephi of old" (D&C 33:8).

The cry is paramount. The scriptures are replete with the counsel that missionaries open their mouths, speak up in confidence, declare the word, make contacts, and not hide their lights under a bushel.

Finding people to teach and singling out those who are ready to listen cannot happen unless you open your mouth and make yourself and your purpose known. Being filled with the spirit of conversion can come only if you are bold to declare that you are on the Lord's errand. Don't fear man more than God! Even though people seem to count God's counsel as worthless or unbelievable, even despising his words — you as a missionary must open your mouth. If you do, people will not only respond and listen, but will also praise you for your courage in bringing them the truth.

The Lord will lead you and be beside you as you go, for He has so declared in the scriptures. Read and ponder these especially selected verses that focus on opening your mouth and speaking up for the cause of the Lord, of truth and righteousness, of goodness and joy.

"And the voice of warning shall be unto all people, by the mouths of my disciples, whom I have chosen in these last days" (D&C 1:4).

"Wherefore, I call upon the weak things of the world, those who are unlearned and despised, to thrash the nations by the power of my Spirit" (D&C 35:13).

"And thou shalt declare glad tidings, yea, publish it upon the mountains, and upon every high place, and among every people that thou shalt be permitted to see.... And of tenets thou shalt not talk, but thou shalt declare repentance and faith on the Savior, and remission of sins by baptism, and by fire, yea, even the Holy Ghost" (D&C 19:29, 31).

"Lift up your voices and spare not. Call upon the nations to repent, both old and young, both bond and free, saying: Prepare yourselves for the great day of the Lord" (D&C 43:20).

"For verily, verily, I say unto you that ye are called to lift up your voices as with the sound of a trump, to declare my gospel unto a crooked and perverse generation" (D&C 33:2).

"Yea, open your mouths and they shall be filled, saying: Repent, repent, and prepare ye the way of the Lord, and make his paths straight; for the kingdom of heaven is at hand; yea, repent and be baptized, every one of you, for a remission of your sins; yea, be baptized even by water, and then cometh the baptism of fire and of the Holy Ghost" (D&C 33:10-11).

PART 4

The Missionary and Self

28

INTEGRITY

Do you write your loved ones the whole truth?

Do you deal with investigators according to what's best for them, not according to your own self-centered record and image?

Are you honest with the storekeeper?

Are you conscientious with your landlord?

Do you spend money frugally, accounting for it carefully?

Do your dealings with the mission president reflect your devotion, your exactness, your diligence?

A missionary goes forth to teach truth to a world practicing half-wisdom and espousing doctrines that are false in the eyes of God. To do God's will, the missionary must be a person of integrity.

Whether the world knows better or not, it needs help. Life can be more beautiful and satisfying. Eternity is a reality. There is purpose in all things under the hand of the master Creator. The Church of Jesus Christ of Latter-day Saints has been given the responsibility in this generation to spread the good news of the fulness of truth, to share the completeness of God's plan for his children, to right the wrongs, to place agency and accountability in line with those laws irrevocably decreed in heaven upon which all blessings are predicated.

The missionary is to help others have the more abundant life.

The missionary must be full of integrity so that those searching for Christ will not be led astray, but will be led to Christ by the complete, sound, unimpaired quality of the truth.

Integrity is more than not lying. It is the letter and the spirit of truth.

Joseph Smith was hated and persecuted for saying that he had seen a vision. In spite of this suffering, he knew he could not deny his sacred experience. He said, "For I had seen a vision; I knew it, and I knew that God knew it, and I could not deny it, neither dared I do it; at least I knew that by so doing I would offend God, and come under condemnation" (Joseph Smith — History 1:25).

Joseph was a man of integrity, no matter what, and the world was changed.

Hyrum Smith was a man of integrity. The Lord said of Hyrum, "Blessed is my servant Hyrum Smith; for I, the Lord, love him because of the integrity of his heart, and because he loveth that which is right before me" (D&C 124:15).

Job held fast to his integrity though his friends and his wife urged him to curse God and die because of all he had lost. No matter what tragedies fell upon Job, he steadfastly lived and proclaimed, "Till I die I will not remove mine integrity from me. My righteousness I hold fast, and will not let it go" (Job 27:5-6).

Job was unwavering in his love of God. Job was a man of integrity, and generations have marveled at and been encouraged by his example.

Mary sat at Jesus' feet while Martha was cumbered with much serving. Jesus responded to Martha's irritability, "One thing is needful: and Mary hath chosen that good part, which shall not be taken away from her" (Luke 10:42). The righteous at last are unfailingly recompensed according to God's will.

The mark of a true disciple of Christ is found within the integrity of his or her own soul. All Elders and Sisters should look within their own souls and see if they are honest with themselves, with the people they teach, with the money they spend in the days of their mission, with the mission president on reports and during interviews, in letters home, in prayers before God.

For example, the money we are given is a sacred trust. Some comes from the General Missionary Fund of the Church (supported by contributions from the Saints worldwide) and some from parents, some from ward members, and some from your own hard work and saving. Even that money is sacred money because the Lord is the giver of all gifts. Yes, we work, but everything is still a gift from God, and unless we look at it that way, we become self-sufficient and self-indulging about our possessions.

Even our communications with others should reflect God's goodness. A missionary of integrity will speak in kindness and truth, with inspirational reminders of God's eternal nature.

If the missionary is not a person of wholeness as his calling would suggest, his efforts cannot be blessed by God. He wastes time and energy and makes a mockery of his sacred assignment.

29

OBEDIENCE

A fter Jesus had performed certain miracles, a woman cried out from the crowd that his mother was a blessed person. Jesus then said, "Yea rather, blessed are they that hear the word of God, and keep it" (Luke 11:28).

How valuable a statement that has been through the history of Christianity!

How relevant obedience is today when there are so many voices in the world crying out to mankind: Behave *this* way, act *that* way, believe *this,* espouse *that,* adhere to *this* alternate principle, support *that* cause, come *here,* go *there.*

Missionaries will be happier and more successful in their important call to serve if they obey God's commandments, the word from Church headquarters, and counsel from their mission president.

You see, a missionary needs help. Missionary work is not a picnic, nor a celebration, nor an easy road.

Missionary work is tough, and the adversary works overtime to tangle, confuse, and drag down the spirit and behavior of the missionary.

A missionary needs blessings.

There is a law that governs how we receive blessings. One doesn't simply pray and wait for God to wave his magic wand to make everything wonderful. The Doctrine and Covenants says it this way: "There is a law, irrevocably decreed in heaven before the foundations of this world, upon which all blessings are predicated — and when we obtain any blessing from God, it is by obedience to that law upon which it is predicated" (D&C 130:20,21).

And again, blessed are they who hear the word (or the law) of God and keep it!

Everything we do is a reflection of our level of obedience to the principles that we value. Stop and think about it: your daily deeds are a reflection of your level of obedience to *your* value system. Your value system should, of course, conform to God's will because blessings are predicated upon his will and word and because we love Him for all He has done for us. So we want to do His will, don't we?

Why would a missionary not want to obey? The answer is clear in the scripture found in Doctrine and Covenants 93:39. The wicked one "cometh and taketh away" light and truth, through disobedience." In other words, when we are disobedient and we allow Satan to fill us with discontent, we are in his domain. We have chosen to draw away from the Lord. The Spirit of God will actually leave us because it cannot be where sin is.

When the Light of Christ leaves us, our decision-making process is thwarted.

We vacillate about right and wrong.

We rationalize ourselves into comfortably breaking rules.

Our power to judge is decreased.

Our happiness and joy are diminished.

Contention increases, because the evil one — the father of all contention — is there taking away the light.

Light from God is an incredible blessing to the missionary. Such light comprehendeth all things, according to Doctrine and Covenants 88:6. Light shows us where and how to go, who is ready to receive the gospel, what approach is appropriate for this person, where danger lurks, what an answer is to a difficult question from an investigator, how to find yourself when you are lost, what to do about a problem with a companion.

Make increased obedience, more exact behavior to the Lord's will, a constant quest. Start with the daily resolve to obey the Lord's will in all things, and gradually this will become a way of life.

In Germany one day, two missionaries had been tracting since early morning. They were bitterly discouraged, and the junior companion wanted to go back to their apartment. They stood at the end of a residential row of housing and discussed their situation. The newer missionary was pleading — he hated tracting, and it had been a total waste of time that whole day. The senior prevailed. He said, "When I came on this mission, I made an agreement with the Lord that I would strive to do his will each day. In fact, we made such an agreement just this morning as we prayed before we left."

"Yes," said the junior companion, "and we've spent hours trying."

"The president asked us to tract until five o'clock P.M. "

"It is almost that time now. Can't we quit?"

"Let's do just this one more street. Okay?" And he started down the row of houses, knocking on the first door. It was one of those times when the Lord had gone before them. The woman who opened the door greeted them warmly and said, "Oh, here you are. I have been waiting for you! Come in!" She told them she had had a dream and had seen their faces exactly and watched them come down the street to her door. She had been doing household work but suddenly felt impressed to look out of her front window — and there came the two young men she had seen in her dream!

She joined the church. What a blessing obedience can be!

30

KNOWLEDGE

How would you feel about having a doctor operate on you with a pair of household scissors?

What about leaving your car to be repaired by a mechanic who knew a little about lawn mowers but nothing about automobiles?

If you signed up for a class in computer science and the teacher turned out to be a barber, how would you react?

There is nothing wrong with a barber, a seamstress with scissors in her hand, or a person who repairs lawn mowers. The point is that when you need an expert in a certain field, you don't want help from an expert in some other field!

When you are dealing with matters of life and death, an expert in religion is welcome. A prophet of God who receives constant inspiration and revelation from God himself is the best blessing for a person seeking answers about life and death.

A missionary is called by such a prophet to help in the Lord's work of bringing answers to people who are searching for truth about life and life after death.

Being a missionary *is* a matter of life and death, so someone who has been called to serve a mission should be serious about his or her preparation. All the rest of somebody's life now and forever may depend on how a certain missionary has prepared. A missionary should be able to teach so that the person will understand, believe, and commit to being baptized.

Now, that missionary may play a great guitar, know how to untangle a sound system, make top grades in university accounting courses, or have operated a financially successful business before retirement, but when a call to serve the Lord as a missionary comes, such experience is not much help. What is needed is skill for sharing truth with an investigator.

Being a missionary is holy service. It deals with God and people and truth and one chance at life! And nobody can teach what they don't know. The work of God requires a godlike person who will learn by study and also by faith.

Joseph Smith said that the moving dedicatory prayer for the Kirtland Temple was given to him by revelation. It includes these relevant words: "As all have not faith, seek ye diligently and teach one another words of wisdom; yea, seek ye out of the best books words of wisdom, *seek learning even by study and also by faith*" (D&C 109:7; italics added).

Examine this further counsel for the missionary and the teacher: "Seek not to declare my word, but first seek to obtain my word" (D&C 11:21). "Seek ye earnestly the best gifts, always remembering for what they are given; for verily I say unto you, they are given for the benefit of those who love me and keep all my commandments, and him that seeketh so to do; that all may be benefited" (D&C 46:8-9).

"Each generation enjoys a vast hoard bequeathed to it by antiquity," wrote Thomas Macaulay. What is learned may be shared, built upon, and experimented with to bring forth additional information. What a missionary is given to teach investigators is truth — the same truth as taught by Adam, Moses, Elijah, Lehi, Nephi, Alma, Mormon, Moroni, Joseph Smith, Brigham Young, and all the succeeding latter-day prophets revealing God's will and his word.

President Antoine R. Ivins was one of the great missionaries of the Church by skill and by calling among the Presidents of the Seventy of the Church. He once gave this mighty perspective in a general conference talk: "If we could teach the world the proper concept of God and Christ and our relationship to them, and do it in such a way that it would sink into their hearts and impel them to study the teachings of the Savior, then apply them in their lives, all these troubles that we worry about now would cease.... Now, we are a small group. It is a tremendous task of remaking the world, but if we are going to have any influence on it, where must we start? I think that we must start with ourselves individually first" (*Improvement Era*, December 1951, p. 889).

The glory of God is intelligence. Not even a missionary can be saved in ignorance of the laws of God, let alone teach them to others. It is helpful to remember always these words: "Whatever principle of intelligence we attain unto in this life, it will rise with us in the resurrection. And if a person gains more knowledge and intelligence in this life through his diligence and obedience than another, he will have so much the advantage in the world to come" (D&C 130:18-19).

You can't teach what you don't know. Keep searching and growing and learning about the gospel. The more you learn, the more incredible, unique, and valuable gospel principles become to you. When certain words fly up at you from the pages of scripture or volumes of lifting literature, know that they are for you. Grasp them to you. Turn them over in your mind. Relate them to your current assignment. Use them to make your time on earth a most blessed period of history.

A missionary need not feel alone in sharing the gospel with others. This is the Lord's work — He will help. But if He has to work through a weakened instrument — a missionary who has not studied, who has not prayed in faith for understanding and retention of the scriptures what do you suppose will happen to that missionary's effectiveness? (And remember that the Spirit will not reside in an unclean vessel.)

Studying the scriptures and learning the missionary approach and discussions will enhance your service with investigators. It also will prepare your spirit to receive inspiration and knowledge through the Holy Ghost! You will be given words to say, directions where to go and whom to approach. Your spirit will be softened, sweetened, and mellowed. This is most desirable for a called servant of the Lord helping others to learn the gospel of Jesus Christ.

A person literally becomes what he or she thinks and feels. A thought that crosses and is retained in the mind will give birth to an act — or an attitude which may speak louder than words or deeds. As a flower springs from the bulb, so a person's mind may be the bulb of his or her being. Cultivated or neglected, either way it produces results.

Which brings us to King Solomon. He prayed for an "understanding heart" (1 Kings 3:9). Through the centuries Solomon has retained the praise of being the wisest of rulers because of his mix of knowledge and a heart that understood.

As a missionary you march beside a band likened to the two thousand sons of Helaman who were prepared to serve. Clinging to the truth that they had learned as children, these Book of Mormon heroes behaved bravely. They marched to war and won without loss of life among their ranks.

A mission demands the best that is in you:
Eyes bright, reflecting clear thinking;
Head cloud-crowned.
You who will not lie or cheat or procrastinate,
Who will not inappropriately best your fellow beings.
You who will resist temptation in any form,
Who can stand like Daniel in the lion's den,
Like Joseph in Liberty Jail silencing the obscenities of the guard.
You who will do what is right, letting whatever consequence
    follow,
Who can keep secrets,
Who can listen with the guarded heart of one who loves his
    fellowmen,
Who can move among people with high principles and hard

work —
Championing the goals of God for his earth children,
Who have studied, memorized, pondered God's word:
To you goes the thrill of lifting others to the level to which
    you have climbed.
You are the prepared servant and will receive his best blessings.

Prepare yourself, for tomorrow the Lord will work wonders among you. "Be ye transformed by the renewing of your mind" (Romans 12:2).

When can you study? When you are on your mission, there are formal hours set aside for study. Make good use of this precious time for your personal growth. Gain the knowledge that will help you bring people to Christ.

Before you go on your mission, life is demanding, but if you try you can find a way to daily secure two hours for this religious preparation. Study when you come in at night. Study during your dinner hour. Get up a half-hour early and study. Let your mind be consumed in the work, and your heart will be ready to receive the promptings of the Spirit.

Then such knowledge you will have!

31

KNOWLEDGE ISN'T ENOUGH

The gospel of Jesus Christ is a wonderful composite of comfort, direction, admonition, and instruction. The gospel provides motivation and impetus for individuals to move forward. Knowing what answers to give in Church classes and being able to recite chapter and verse in the scriptures is a great achievement. However, only if a person also actively applies the principles of the gospel to his life is the Lord's plan being fulfilled for the benefit of mankind.

There are two truths to keep in mind.

One, knowledge of the gospel is imperative because people cannot be exalted in ignorance. Whatever intelligence we gain in this life will be part of our being and rise with us in the resurrection (see D&C 130:18).

Two, exaltation depends on our living by the word of God. Wise is the person who will awake and arouse his or her faculties and experiment upon the word, actually applying God's principles to daily living.

Solomon was King David's son. When Solomon became king of all Israel, God appeared to him in the night and asked Solomon what gift he desired. Solomon replied, "Give me now wisdom and knowledge" (2 Chronicles 1:10). Solomon wanted to judge the people fairly and move before them having

---

within himself the power of God, who loves all people.

God gave wisdom to Solomon because "thou hast not asked riches, wealth, or honour, nor the life of thine enemies, neither yet hast asked long life; but hast asked wisdom and knowledge for thyself" (2 Chronicles 1:11).

Solomon's experience is a reminder to those called to serve that they should seek wisdom as well as knowledge to make their service indeed beneficial to others. We study, learn, and seek out of the best books, all the while humbly praying for understanding and wisdom. Then, through the power of the Holy Ghost, the heavens will be opened, knowledge will pour down from heaven, and the soul will be greatly enlarged (see D&C 121:45).

Knowledge is not enough for any situation. For example, people know how babies are made, and still a staggering number of illegitimate infants come into the world. Mistakes are made. Knowledge hasn't been enough to forestall a problem. Many, many hearts are broken as a result.

People know that eating too much of the wrong foods produces fat in the body. Yet the world is crowded with overweight people who receive shocking news standing on the scales and often suffer the sad consequences of disease and low self-esteem. Knowledge doesn't always control behavior.

People know that dishonesty is against the law of God and the law of the land. But knowledge isn't enough to protect against temptation. Proof of this is in the increasing number of incidents of lying, cheating, robberies, scams, gambling, prostitution, murders, and all manner of situations where people offend and take advantage of others.

Some people may say that they know God lives and that the gospel is true, and yet they persist in ungodlike activity on a greater or lesser scale. Some may listen to the prophet speak, but then take issue with his counsel. Some may teach a lesson on faith, but when a loved one dies, they weep and wail and cry, "Why me?"

Knowledge alone doesn't get us into heaven. We need understanding and wisdom, and we need to use them to make life more satisfying for ourselves and others.

If we lack knowledge and wisdom, we but need to ask God (see D&C 42:68; James 1:5). Joseph Smith did just that, and look what knowledge and understanding he received to benefit all mankind!

An important teaching of the Lord was, "And why call ye me, Lord, Lord, and do not the things which I say? Whosoever cometh to me, and heareth my sayings, and doeth them, I will shew you to whom he is like: he is like a man which built an house, and digged deep, and laid the foundation on a rock: and when the flood arose, the stream beat vehemently upon that house, and could not shake it: for it was founded upon a rock. But he that heareth, and doeth not, is like a man that without a foundation built an house upon the earth; against which the stream did beat vehemently, and immediately it fell; and the ruin of that house was great" (Luke 6:46 49).

Remember, oh, remember, that "the wise in heart will receive commandments" — accept the word of God and live by it — rather than suffer the consequences of not doing so (Proverbs 10:8).

There is a well-known legend about three who went to heaven at the same time and were interviewed by the gate-keeper. The first was asked, "What think ye of Christ?" And the first showed his great knowledge of the scriptures as he replied, "O chapter and verse, chapter and verse!"

"I see," said the gatekeeper. "Step right over here."

The second stepped forward to be interviewed by the gatekeeper and was asked the same question, "What think ye of Christ?" And the second person listed her credentials of service, "O sacred casserole, sacred casserole, cake for the funeral meal, cookies for the missionaries."

"I see," said the gatekeeper. "Step right over here."

Then the third was beckoned before the gatekeeper. "What think ye of Christ?" And the third fell at His feet and worshiped Him, for he knew the Savior.

To those called to serve, knowledge is seldom sufficient to do the Lord's work. Along with all your studying and memorizing, praying for understanding and wisdom is imperative. A witness of Jesus Christ gained through the power of the Holy Ghost will add power and strength to your teaching.

32

GRATITUDE

The Lord has said, "In nothing doth man offend God, or against none is his wrath kindled, save those who confess not his hand in all things, and obey not his commandments" (D&C 59:21).

We learn in life that if the blessings showered upon man are received with a thankful heart, that proves or shows his love for God. Gratitude becomes an essential part of a Christlike life.

Missionaries come to love King Benjamin's sermon because there is so much truth and wisdom in it that it frequently is used for teaching investigators. In terms of the quality of gratitude that can enhance every missionary, we turn to this sermon:

> And behold also, if I, whom ye call your king, who has spent his days in your service, and yet has been in the service of God, do merit any thanks from you, O how you ought to thank your heavenly King!
>
> I say unto you, my brethren, that if you should render all the thanks and praise which your whole soul has power to possess, to that God who has created you, and has kept and preserved you, and has caused that ye should rejoice, and has granted that ye should live in peace one with another —

I say unto you that if ye should serve him who has created you from the beginning, and is preserving you from day to day, by lending you breath, that ye may live and move and do according to your own will, and even supporting you from one moment to another — I say, if ye should serve him with all your whole souls yet ye would be unprofitable servants (Mosiah 2:19-21).

Before you pray to Heavenly Father again, ask yourself some searching questions, perhaps like the following:

1. Have I thanked my family for their support, their love through the years of preparation for a mission, their insightful correction of my weakness, their financial investment, their patience, their ways of making me feel worthwhile and secure, and hundreds of other things they have done and continue to do for me?

2. Am I an appreciative partner to my companion in the mission field? Have I said thanks for the thousand kindnesses and courtesies he or she shows me?

3. Did I thank the bishopric of the ward at home for their letters of support and reports on ward happenings, as well as for their specific help in getting me on a mission?

4. Did I thank the Lord for health, strength, food, shelter, and protection in the mission field — and throughout my life?

5. Have I openly recognized the talents God has given me and thanked him for these things, asking him to help me use them well for his work?

6. Have I remembered to acknowledge his hand in convert baptisms and for special help with the Holy Spirit during teaching meetings?

7. On Fast Sunday did I have a fast of gratitude for success with the work, and a prayer and fast for those being taught the gospel?

8. Have I thanked the Lord for members' help?

9. Have I thanked the members themselves in warmth and sincerity?

10. Did I thank the Lord for letting me be an instrument in his hands in bringing souls to understand him and his plan?

In pondering your life, in pondering your daily prayer, you may find room for improvement in showing forth your gratitude to others important to your life. How much more, as King Benjamin said, should you be grateful to God!

We can show gratitude in many ways. We can be positive, smile, and say please and thank you as nice children are taught to. These are basic traits of gratitude. What about counting blessings in your journal? Write down every joyful blessing and comfort of life. Then find appropriate ways of expressing sincere thanks to those responsible for your well-being.

33

CLEANLINESS

Do you know that your chances of being hit by a car in the United States is one in twenty thousand? With the enormous population of people and cars in America these days, your chance of risk comes around quickly.

Keep watchful.

Also, keep clean — your life is at risk!

There are frightening statistics that might be related about the life-threatening incidents in connection with smoking, drinking, poor health habits, sexual sin on any level, and not taking proper care of your body, which not so incidentally is a temple of God because it houses your eternal spirit created by Heavenly Father. Here are some cautions.

As a missionary you may move from the protected society of a small Mormon town, from the sociality of a supportive branch for worship and activity, from a house kept spotless and clothing kept laundered by a diligent mother, from an environment with few worldly temptations. You may meet with "nice" and "bright" people who do not keep the high standards espoused by The Church of Jesus Christ of Latter-day Saints. You may wish you had learned personal cleanliness of body and soul before you left home to preach of Christ in the world!

It could save your eternal life and make life on earth more worthwhile, as well. Wisely did the Lord counsel, "Cease to be idle; cease to be unclean" (D&C 88:124).

There is an old adage, "Cleanliness is next to Godliness." There is much truth in that saying. No unclean thing can enter the kingdom of God. The Holy Ghost cannot enter an unclean person. (Nor an unclean bedroom!)

"Behold, mine house is a house of order, saith the Lord God, and not a house of confusion" (D&C 132:8).

Life is at risk when you drink, smoke, practice poor health habits, give in to lust, allow slovenly habits of self and soul to become the pattern, and withdraw from God, turning away from the sacred things you know to be true. It is then that a person can become beyond feeling.

In a remarkable father-son moment recorded in Alma 37, Alma pointed out to his son Helaman that the Liahona instrument that guided their fathers from Jerusalem to the American continent "did work for them according to their faith in God." If they were slothful and forgot to exercise their faith and diligence, "then those marvelous works ceased, and they did not progress in their journey...and were afflicted...because of their transgressions." Then Alma said to Helaman, "O my son, do not let us be slothful because of the easiness of the way; for so was it with our fathers; for so was it prepared for them, that if they would look they might live; even so it is with us. The way is prepared, and if we will look we may live forever" (Alma 37:3846).

The sweet counsel of God has no place in the heart or lifestyle of someone who does not have the companionship of the Holy Ghost, who has rejected the Lord, who has not ordered his or her life, who is not clean after the manner of the Lord's will.

A Latter-day Saint serving a mission in the name of Jesus Christ, having been called to serve and set apart from the world for a specific period of time to do sacred service, ought to "be an example of the believers." Paul wrote to Timothy these insistent and important words that have close connection to the situation of a missionary today: "Be thou an example of the believers, in word, in conversation, in charity, in spirit, in faith, in purity.... Neglect not the gift that is in thee, which was given thee by prophecy, with the laying on of the hands" (1 Timothy 4:12,14).

As you keep your soiled laundry hidden and separate from your clean clothing, so you will remove any soiling-to-the-soul habit or thought that would threaten your personal purity. To do otherwise is to put your whole life at risk.

Keep watchful.

Keep clean.

34

HUMILITY

Called to serve Him! Imagine, you are in the service of the Lord Jesus Christ!

You are not just called to serve the sick and afflicted or the people who haven't been blessed yet by the fulness of the gospel or the members of the local branch. You understand that when you have "done it unto the least" of God's children, you have served him.

But a mission is a unique call. When you are formally called, set apart, and under holy inspiration assigned to a specific field of missionary labor, you become his special agent, his special disciple called to help in a particular way and place to do his work. Say it again — it is the effort to bring to pass the immortality and eternal life of man; to spread the gospel, the good news; to bring people to Christ; to teach people how to live and grow, to be happy and more pure; to get people ready for heaven, which is life in Heavenly Father's presence.

Such an important call! Such an awesome assignment! There is so much to learn and so little time to get ready. If you're like most missionaries, suddenly humility is the overwhelming feeling.

Over and over again you think: it is my mission to help with his mission. This work is the purpose of earth life. And you are now officially *on his team!* It isn't a two-year vacation, after all, or a study abroad kind of opportunity. Suddenly you see it all. This is your call to *serve Him.* This is your chance, your blessed opportunity.

The reality of it sweeps you. You melt. You sink to your knees. Your heart is pounding, and your head naturally bows as you understand who God is, whose errand you are on — you spill it all out in prayer. "Father, I don't know enough. I've never been very far away from home. I am frightened. I am resisting this change. I am worried about my sins and weaknesses. Wilt thou forgive me? Can I get along with my companion? Will the mission president like me? Will I like him and his wife? Will I like the place I am assigned? What about the climate, the food, the cost? And how can anybody as unprepared spiritually and mentally as I am be of any use? I've barely read the Book of Mormon. I don't listen enough in church. Oh, Father, help me. Help me."

All of a sudden warmth flushes throughout your body. You feel the Spirit of the Lord. Incredible! You know that He is there with you. You know that He knows you are there! Your prayer has reached heaven. You will be all right.

There is a great story from the Bible that teaches a helpful lesson to someone humble enough to rely upon the Lord. It is found in Mark 9. A worried father brought his sorely stricken son before the Lord and asked that the Lord heal the lad. "Jesus said unto him, If thou canst believe, all things are possible to him that believeth. And straightway the father of the child cried out, and said with tears, Lord, I believe; help thou mine unbelief" (Mark 9:23-24).

The boy was healed, and the throngs of people and the disciples of Christ marveled. Two things in this story to remember: (1) the Lord can do all things and (2) when your own faith isn't strong enough, admit to Christ, "Help thou mine unbelief."

Humility is essential to successful service in the Lord's kingdom. He can work wonders through someone willing to call upon him for an understanding of his will; enlightenment about his principles; strength against the adversary; confidence in the face of enemies; endurance in times of trial; comfort and peace; and fortitude to work tirelessly with all your heart, might, mind, and strength!

Humility is an essential requisite of all who are called to serve Him. "No one can assist in this work except he shall be humble and full of love, having faith, hope, and charity, being temperate in all things, whatsoever shall be entrusted to his care" (D&C 12:8; see also D&C 4:6; Ether 12:27).

35

Beyond Reproach

One of the better things about serving as a missionary is the frequent opportunity to evaluate yourself and see if you are beyond reproach. Personal evaluations have a way of showing up positive qualities as well as some slightly negative tendencies.

As you continually evaluate yourself — beginning now — you start with your head and check to see if it is "on straight," as the saying goes. Is your mind programmed to keep you moving along the straight and narrow? Is your mind in control of your life, your choices, your reactions, your actions? Or are you kicked by emotions — easy to anger, easy to self-pity, easy to have hurt feelings, quick to be jealous or even resentful of another's success?

Every missionary is set apart so that he or she may be enhanced by the Spirit of God — that is, be even better at this work than he or she might naturally be. Think of the words Paul the Apostle wrote to Timothy, whom he considered his dearly beloved son: "Wherefore I put thee in remembrance that thou stir up the gift of God, which is in thee by the putting on of my hands. For God hath not given us the spirit of fear; but of power, and of love, and of a sound mind" (2 Timothy 1:6-7).

Now as part of this important self-evaluation, move to your

heart. Look deep inside. What do you see? Consider the questions listed in Alma 5 in terms of your own life and feelings.

> And now behold, I ask of you, my brethren of the church, have ye spiritually been born of God? Have ye received his image in your countenances? Have ye experienced this mighty change in your hearts?

> Do ye exercise faith in the redemption of him who created you? Do you look forward with an eye of faith, and view this mortal body raised in immortality, and this corruption raised in incorruption, to stand before God to be judged according to the deeds which have been done in the mortal body? (Alma 5:14-15).

These revealing verses are but a fraction of the wise counsel and questioning that is stirred up in one who reads Alma 5 and matches self against the high standards considered in that chapter.

It is agreed that none of us is perfect, although we hope to become so one day. Meanwhile the ideal missionary, the devoted disciple, wants to be above reproach.

Here are some questions relating to that goal. Ask yourself:

1. Do I ever speak light-mindedly about my investigators?
2. Do I use nicknames for my investigators that might be considered disrespectful?
3. Do I seek only a certain kind of investigator?
4. Do I proselyte only one area rather than giving all people a chance to hear the gospel?
5. Do I respect time?
   - Do I visit too long with members?
   - Do I stay too late with investigators?
   - Do I come in too late?
   - Do I show up late for church?

- Do I arrive too early for dinner with members?

6. Am I honest in my work?
   - Are my reports accurate?
   - Do I skimp on study time and skill training?

7. Am I honest in the handling of money?
   - Do I pay my share of the telephone bill? other shared bills?
   - Do I overdraft? If so, why?

8. Do I guard my speech?
   - Do I take the Lord's name in vain?
   - Do I ever swear or use obscenities in any form?
   - Do I keep confidences?
   - Do I broadcast the problems of others?
   - Do I make public fun of my companion?
   - Do I talk too openly about my own problems?

9. Do I keep my interviews with the mission president confidential?

10. Do I sustain and support the General Authorities of the Church and the mission president and refuse to criticize or speak disrespectfully in any way?

11. Do I spend too much time with the opposite sex, flirt, or show improper affection ever?

12. Am I truly trying to live beyond reproach, thus setting myself up for the companionship and guidance of the Holy Ghost?

Missionaries are happy when they are beyond reproach. They enjoy success. They wax confident before God and feel his approbation. They think of others before themselves and virtue garnishes their thoughts.

36

Overcoming Fear

L ife is full of growing experiences that teach us to overcome opposition, obstacles, weaknesses, and often fear.
We must overcome the fear of man in many aspects of missionary work — knocking on doors, using "the survey," and
even asking the "golden question." We overcome this fear as
we do the following:

- Build and strengthen our faith in God (Helaman 3:35).

- Wax strong in our knowledge and testimony of the
  truth (Alma 17:2-3).

- Increase the love of Christ in our hearts (1 John 4:18,
  Moroni 8:16).

- Practice our skills so we may grow in confidence (1
  Nephi 3:7).

- Remember the Atonement (D&C 20:77, 79).

By maintaining a strong assurance of the truth of the gospel,
being firm in our faith in God, and developing in our hearts the
divine love of Christ for our fellowmen, we can become more
concerned for others' eternal welfare than for our own comfort,
just as Ammon and the sons of Mosiah when they went to teach
the Lamanites. Faith and love will replace fear.

Fear can be a result of sin. Guilt often brings with it a fear
of the consequences of sin. An early result of Adam's trans-
gression was a feeling of fear and self-consciousness. Often,
the guilty not only do not want to talk to the Lord, but also

cannot even stand to be in his presence (see Alma 12:14).

When we do wrong, do poorly, are disobedient, make a horrible mistake, fail to do our duty, let others down, or commit sins of varying degrees, we experience an interesting fear-related phenomenon in our response to our leaders. Whether our leader is a parent, an employer, a home teaching supervisor, a bishop, a mission president, or a zone leader, our reaction is usually the same: when we are not doing what we know we should, we do not like to talk to our leaders or to those with stewardship responsibility over us. We sometimes try to transfer our guilt to our leaders. We blame them for our failure and literally become angry with our Heavenly Father or with our leaders, saying negative things such as, "Where were they when I needed them?"; "This was a stupid thing to do anyway"; "They have required a hard thing of me"; "I never did like them"; or "I don't care."

To avoid this phenomenon, we must (1) take responsibility for our own attitudes and actions, (2) choose to be easily entreated (humble), (3) choose to be positive about the need to improve, and (4) look at leaders as helpers. *Remember, we only become angry or fearful when we refuse to admit our guilt and attempt to cover it by blaming another person or circumstance for our predicament and negative feelings.* Placing the blame outside of ourselves is an attempt to deceive ourselves into believing that we are not responsible for the problem, and therefore do not need to change. When we do not want to change, or feel that we do not *need* to change, we perceive our leaders as a threat to our "comfort zone." If we will admit our faults, change anything in ourselves that needs changing, and try always to follow the path of righteousness, we can avoid these negative attitudes and feelings.

We can overcome fear. The Lord has told us the way. We can feel secure in all we do, through personal righteousness and humility before the Lord (see D&C 121:45). As we overcome fear and fill our lives with righteousness and faith, we will be filled with the Spirit of the Lord, and we will teach with great power (see Alma 26:22).

37

STEADFASTNESS

Nephi exemplified well the ability to persevere and to work with unwearyingness:

> Blessed art thou, Nephi, for those things which thou hast done; for I have beheld how thou hast with unwearyingness declared the word, which I have given unto thee, unto this people. And thou hast not feared them, and has not sought thine own life, but hast sought my will, and to keep my commandments.
>
> And now, because thou hast done this with such unwearyingness, behold, I will bless thee forever; and I will make thee mighty in word and in deed, in faith and in works; yea, even that all things shall be done unto thee according to thy word, for thou shalt not ask that which is contrary to my will. (Helaman 10:4-5.)

Throughout his entire life, Nephi submitted himself to the will of the Father and worked continually to build the kingdom of God. How can you become like Nephi? Here are a few guidelines:

1. Build a relationship with the Savior based on gratitude and love. Let your mind be consumed with the glory of God and with his will, and your love and gratitude will show in your obedience and performance.

2. Obtain the vision of the work and the desire to achieve;

pay the price to prepare; be enthused and excited continually; make goals, plans, and commitments; and gain self-mastery through personal discipline; and you shall succeed in becoming a steadfast missionary. Study and skill-training take discipline and vision.

3. Acquire a character like unto Ammon when he received strength from the Lord to do all things. His character was a result of consistency in being exactly obedient.

4. Apply the principles of baptism and recognize the reasons underlying them, so that you internalize them and behave as true disciples of Christ, thus becoming mighty instruments in the hands of God.

5. Work one day at a time — don't get overwhelmed. Make your goals and plans for the week, and then simply do one-seventh of them a day, steadily bettering your best.

6. Purify your life through repentance so you can be led by the Spirit (see 1 Nephi 4:6).

7. Rejoice in doing the work and in doing it well, and you will then continue in the way of the Lord because of the joy of doing so.

Don't try to be happy and enjoy life when you are not doing your best — you can't. We deceive ourselves if we think we can feel good when we fail to follow our leaders or when we choose to set up our own rules for our behavior. When we are disobedient, our desire to work leaves us, our enthusiasm and excitement wanes, and we feel disheartened when people reject our message.

There is only one way to be happy, to enjoy our mission, and that is by living a disciplined life built on steadfastness to God's work and by being exactly obedient. Success is yours for the having. Righteousness is happiness. As you dedicate yourself to being a faithful, steadfast missionary, you will be happy, for this is the design of existence.

38

Self-Mastery

One element of a great character is discipline or self-mastery. The word *discipline* comes from the same root as the word *disciple*. A truly disciplined person is a disciple, a believer, one whose heart is changed so that it is his nature to keep the commandments. A disciplined person will improve for Jesus' sake (his improvement becomes his gift to his Savior), has a sense of stewardship towards life, and is ready to sacrifice and serve.

Self-discipline thwarts temptation. Disciplined people master their moods and subordinate the body to the spirit so the mind and spirit direct behavior. They are steady and reliable. Their reasons for righteousness prevail long after flashing emotions are past. Disciplined people apply true principles — prayer, preparation, diligence, and so on (see D&C 4) — to win the race of life. The exercise of true discipline prepares them to receive and obey the promptings of the Spirit. People with true discipline serve others and bless lives in a divine way.

Character without discipline is weak; people need discipline in order to reach their full potential. Failure to achieve reachable goals may reveal a lack of discipline, and excuses only indicate aversion to restraint and control. Rebellion against discipline — evidenced by attitudes of insubordination, selfishness, misery, and uselessness will disease the heart and prevent the exercise of discipline and faith. Much lack of discipline comes from seeking a good time rather than God's will. Such misplaced priorities often make discipline seem a burden.

When a person's heart and goals are in tune with the Spirit, he accepts discipline and rules graciously. A disciplined person knows that boundaries make it possible for him to be productive within his sphere. Laws bring standards to obey, and obedience brings the blessings of heaven.

Here are some ways to receive the blessings that accompany self-discipline:

1. Put your priorities in order. Seek God's will first.
2. Avoid shortcuts. Be truly willing to do what is required.
3. Submit to mission rules rather than doing as you please and then asking for forgiveness.
4. Keep your "needs" in perspective, especially when talking with your leaders.
5. Begin with discipline in simple things, such as getting up and out on time and studying.
6. Be punctual. Courtesy demands it.
7. Respect time. Use it well.
8. Do difficult things first — promptly. Be independent of moods, especially those that tempt you to say, "I don't feel like it"
9. Train and subordinate your body — the hands, the eyes, the movements.
10. Control your appetite and conquer poor eating habits (including both under- and overeating).
11. Control your tongue. Say nothing negative. Do not indulge in backbiting, complaining, or evil-speaking.
12. Gird up your mind. Think positive thoughts and refuse to allow negative ones.

13. Stop worrying — it is folly. Do something positive instead.

14. If you are not having success, ponder and learn from disappointments. Take advantage of problems, and thank God for trials.

15. Receive instruction, correction, or chastisement humbly and gratefully, and learn from it.

16. Avoid prejudgment and dogmatism.

17. Cultivate a sense of responsibility.

18. Pray.

Remember always that discipline is a tool, a servant, to help you do the Lord's will, it is not a savior or an end in itself. Discipline will give you increased capacity for and dedication to the task at hand, whether it be preparing, gaining skills, practicing self-mastery, or simply keeping commitments. Discipline produces the joy of righteous living — happiness and success. If you will exercise discipline with love in your heart, living and teaching by the Spirit, you will enjoy the strength of the Lord, and you will build the habits of Christlike character: you will be Christlike (see 3 Nephi 27:27), and you will be blessed abundantly.

39

OUR WILL TO DO RIGHT

Do we have insurmountable problems? At times we think we do, but they are really an opportunity to exercise our faith and our will to do right.

We often think that the causes of our problems and lack of success are outside of ourselves, and thus we look outside of ourselves for the solutions. This is wrong thinking. *There are no external solutions to internal problems.* Although we may think that our problems are caused by our circumstances, leaders, companions, language, area, ward, or anything or anybody else, we deceive ourselves if we don't realize that frequently it is we who need to change, repent, purify ourselves, keep our commitments and covenants, and increase in Christlike love. The solution is in us and in the teachings of Christ.

In the gospel of Christ, nearly all commandments are stated positively; that is, we are told what to do instead of what not to do, with the overriding positive promise that the sure way to avoid evil is to do good. Our gospel teaching will have power only when we live the great positive principles we teach: faith in the Lord and in his gospel, repentance, change, a broken heart and a contrite spirit, and exact obedience to the will of Christ. The gospel is the most positive philosophy of all time. Its message is that we *can* change, through Christ, its author, who was and is the most positive being of all time.

Who but this kind of optimist would want his disciples, even as he awaited crucifixion, to have joy (see John 15:11), and who would teach them so powerfully that they would never forget? Even after his death, his disciples took food with gladness (Acts 2:46), rejoiced when they suffered shame for his name (Acts 5:41), sang and rejoiced in the jails of Rome (Philippians 4:4; Acts 16:25), and taught that the fruits of the Spirit were love, joy, and peace (Galatians 5:22). When Paul dreamed of the departed Master, he heard the Lord say to His disciples, "Be of good cheer." The Lord was the Bridegroom, the bringer of joy, who told us to rejoice when we are persecuted for His sake, to leap for joy, to look happy when we are fasting, and to be exceeding glad. It was He who revealed to Lehi that "men are, that they might have joy" (2 Nephi 2:25).

How did He meet problems? With unfailing optimism. Even when the odds to mortal eyes seemed overwhelming, the Savior never doubted His purpose: the possibility of failure never crossed His mind. In his teachings and parables, good always prevailed. In his ongoing work, also, good always prevails. He is master of causing even the bleakest of situations to turn out for the best. His life and teachings radiate purpose and the assurance of ultimate success. To have this assurance and joy, remember His omnipotence, love, and total reliability, and do the following:

1. Eliminate all negative and critical moments.
2. Focus your speech and thoughts on missionary work only, even in your letters home.
3. Try to exercise greater faith and mentally visualize yourself being successful.
4. Emphasize the positive in every situation.
5. Make a sign to put in your apartment which reminds you to be positive.
6. Help your companion when your speech begins turning to worldly issues.

7. Read the following scriptures: Luke 6:23; Matthew 6:16-18; Matthew 5:12; 2 Nephi 9:18; Job 38:7; Psalms 30:5; Isaiah 35:10; Matthew 13:20; 2 Corinthians 2:3; and 1 Peter 1:8.

8. Overcome negative feelings by seeking in all things to do what you know and feel is right.

PART 5

THE MISSIONARY AND THE GRAND VISION

40

ACCORDING TO THE PROPHETS

So you are going on a mission! Wonderful! You surely will want to know as much as you can about missionary work. No perspective on a Church subject is complete without the view of prophets — each, in his own day, a mouthpiece of God. The word of a prophet is invaluable to a missionary, indeed to anyone who wants to grow in the gospel and share it with others.

Read the words of the following prophets (in the first instance, the Lord speaking through Joseph Smith) with your current needs in mind. Digest these inspired thoughts, and let them fuel your desire to understand your assignment and to further ready yourself for the time when you are formally called to serve.

JOSEPH SMITH

"And the voice of warning shall be unto all people, by the mouths of my disciples, whom I have chosen in these last days.

"And they shall go forth and none shall stay them, for I the Lord have commanded them" (D&C 1:4-5).

EZRA TAFT BENSON

"The time must surely come when the Iron Curtain will be melted down and the Bamboo Curtain shattered. What the Lord has decreed will be fulfilled. To members of the Church and honest-hearted people everywhere, we remind you that God is at the helm — he is not dead — and he has said, 'Be still, and know that I am God' (Psalm 46:10)...

"To the thousands throughout the world who are accepting the gospel; to faithful missionaries everywhere and devoted families who support them: go forward with faith and courage. You are engaged in the greatest work in all the world — the saving of the souls of the children of men. In this great work we cannot fail" (*Improvement Era*, June 1970, p. 96).

SPENCER W. KIMBALL

"In 1834, a high council was being organized by the Prophet Joseph Smith. This account comes from L. D. Young:

"'...I committed a grave error, and desire to leave a record of it, for a lesson to others. The prophet requested me to take a seat with the brethren who had been selected for this [high] council. Instead of doing so, I arose and pled my inability to fill so responsible a position, manifesting, I think, considerable earnestness in the matter.

"'The prophet then said he merely desired I should take the place; but as I still excused myself, he appointed another to fill it. I think this was the reason that he never again called me to fill any important position in the priesthood. I have since learned to go where I am called, and not set up my judgment against that of those who are called to guide in this kingdom.'...

"'Remember the four things come not back: the spoken word, the sped arrow, the past life, and the neglected opportunity (Marden, p.67)....

"The world is full of opportunities missed. Many of the impressive talks of this conference have told of people who failed to accept the gospel when presented; of dropouts from high school, college, and employment, of waste through drugs and immoralities; of failures to accept Church and community service; of bypassing a proselyting mission; of a temporary civil marriage substituted for a permanent eternal one; of the use of the pill, abortion, and other means of damaging or destroying the family and home life so strongly urged as vital to our continued civilization. All this reminds us that though we must be in the world, we need not be of the world" (in Conference Report, October 1970, pp. 70-72).

HAROLD B. LEE

"A few years ago a man came here in our midst and said to one of our brethren, 'If you people would do away with one principle in your belief, I could join the Church tomorrow.' And our brother asked, 'What is that principle?'

"He replied, 'If you would do away with your belief in present-day revelation, I could join your church.'

"Then an amazing statement was made to me by our brother, the man who was the Church member: 'You know, I think we ought to do something about that.'

"...Whenever we come to a time where we begin to deny that there is revelation to this church, it is tantamount to saying that we believe that the power of God does not exist in our midst today. We must believe and know for a certainty and have a sure testimony that God does reveal, and is now revealing, all things pertaining to his kingdom today, as in every other dispensation.

"...The greatest danger among us today is fear. Fear doesn't come of the Lord. Faith and peace are the fruits of the Spirit. May we teach our people where to look to for peace — not peace that can be legislated in the halls of Congress or be maintained by armies and navies and tanks and guns and airplanes, but peace that can come as the Master said it would come, by overcoming the things of the world" (*Improvement Era,* June 1970, p. 65).

JOSEPH FIELDING SMITH

"Procrastination, as it may be applied to gospel principles, is the thief of eternal life, which is life in the presence of the Father and the Son. There are many among us, even members of the Church, who feel that there is no need for haste in the observance of gospel principles and the keeping of the commandments....

"To enter the celestial [kingdom] and obtain exaltation, it is necessary that the whole law be kept....

"'And I give unto you a commandment that you shall teach one another the doctrine of the kingdom' (D&C 88:76-77)" (in Conference Report, April 1969, pp. 121-23).

DAVID O. MCKAY

"Ours is the responsibility — greater than ever before:

"1. To proclaim that the Church was divinely established by the appearance of God the Father and his Son Jesus Christ to the Prophet Joseph Smith, and that divine authority through the priesthood is given to represent Deity in establishing Christ's Church upon the earth.

"2. To proclaim that its assigned responsibility to fulfill the admonition of Jesus to his apostles: 'Go ye therefore, and teach all nations, baptizing them in the name of the Father, and of the Son, and of the Holy Ghost:

"'Teaching them to observe all things whatsoever I have commanded you: and, lo, I am with you alway, even unto the end of the world. Amen.' (Matthew 28:19-20.)

"3. To proclaim peace and goodwill unto all mankind.

"4. To exert every effort and all means within our reach to make evil-thinking men good, and good men better, and all people happier.

"5. To proclaim the truth that each individual is a child of God and important in his sight....

"We are all missionaries. We may drop a word here, bear our testimony, be an exemplar by what we do; and, as we accept this call and discharge our duties in the stakes, wards, quorums, and the mission field, our acts will 'roll from soul to soul and go forever and forever'" (in Conference Report, October 1969, pp. 8687).

GEORGE ALBERT SMITH

"I remember one day I was impressed to say to a missionary who was going to a certain town where they would not let us hold street meetings:

"'Now remember, give the Lord a chance. You are going to ask a favor. Give the Lord a chance. Ask Him to open the way.'

"The young man went to that city, went into the office of the mayor, and asked if he could see him. He was going to ask if they might change the rule.

"When he got there, he found that the mayor was out of town. The young man came out of the office, looked down the hall and saw on a door at the end of the hall, 'Chief Constable's Office.' He hesitated a moment, and something said to him: 'Give the Lord a chance.' He walked into the chief constable's office and told him what he had come for. When he finished the man said:

"'Well, what street corner would you like?'

"He said: 'I don't know this city as well as you do. I would not ask for a corner that would be undesirable, or where we would block the traffic. Would you mind going with me to select a corner?'

"Just think of a missionary asking the chief constable to pick a corner on which to preach the gospel!

"The constable said:

"'Surely, I will go with you.'

"In fifteen minutes they had one of the best corners in town, with permission to preach the gospel of Jesus Christ where it had not been preached on the streets....

"The Lord has a way of accomplishing things that we are unable to do, and he never asks us to do anything that he does not make the way possible" (*Improvement Era*, July 1946, p. 427).

HEBER J. GRANT

"There is no dividend that any human being can draw from bonds or stocks, or anything in the wealth of the world, that compares with the knowledge in one's heart that he or she has been an instrument in the hands of God of shaping some life for good....

"I know that many times I have poured out the gratitude of my heart to...the teacher of my Sunday School class in my boyhood and young manhood days. I shall never get over thanking this man for the wonderful impression for good that he made upon me and for the remarkable testimonies he bore in our classes, telling his experiences as a missionary, and the blessings and power of God that attended him while proclaiming the Gospel on two missions to his native country, Scotland....

"...The important thing for you is to have a love of your work and to do your work under the inspiration of the Spirit of the living God. That is the whole difference between the Church of Jesus Christ and the people of the world. They have the letter of the Gospel; they are teaching the Bible just as diligently and many of them believe in it as strongly and try to live up to its precepts just as well as we do; but the Spirit of the living God they do not have. Why? Because they haven't the power of the Priesthood, and because they have not accepted [the fulness of] the Gospel as we have" (*Improvement Era*, March 1939, p. 135).

JOSEPH F. SMITH

"All Latter-day Saints certainly recognize that the Church is greater than any man, and must be considered in all cases in preference to individuals. Men pass away, but the Church, the cause of God, remains permanently. Loyalty to the Church is one of the characteristics of the Latter-day Saints. They do not count too great any necessary sacrifice when rendered for its benefit. Every good Latter-day Saint is willing to do his share toward its advancement. Hundreds of missionaries are called each year; they go out into the world for two, three or more years, occupy positions in their various fields of labor, and when their work is complete, their places are filled by new men, and they return home to take up other work and duties. They do not feel that their release, when they have done faithful work, is at all unwelcome or undesirable" (*Improvement Era*, July 1907, p. 752).

41

TWO BATTLES

W hen you have been called to serve a mission for The Church of Jesus Christ of Latter-day Saints, you will soon find that a certain kind of war has been declared: Satan wants you to fail, and Heavenly Father wants to ensure your success.

It is commonly understood and oft repeated that each time ground is broken for a new temple, all the bells in hell begin to ring and Satan's troops are called into specifc action — all of which indicates the importance of temples!

The same is true in missionary work. Satan, still angry from losing the War in Heaven, now wages damage among those called to serve as missionaries. The adversary is real, and he is active. Since the War in Heaven between the forces of evil and the followers of Christ, Satan accepts any progress on the Lord's side as a kind of declaration of war.

When trouble comes, the Saints must rally their forces.

The battleground will not only be in the mission field and among the people you are called specifically to serve, but within yourself as well.

Two battles.

Be warned. Get ready for two battles. One is the battle within, and the other is the battle outside yourself.

Both must be won. You want to resist inner workings of

temptations, and you want to rise above difficulties imposed by the world outside yourself.

THE BATTLE WITHIN

The battle within may take on a variety of appearances. Here are a few to watch out for:

- Strange places, strange people, strange language, strange food
- Homesickness
- Companions reared differently from you
- Restrictions in life-style
- Feelings of inadequacy
- Loneliness
- Confusion and depression
- Thoughts that nobody will ever know if you slip a little
- Fabricated reports to the mission president
- Patterns of rationalizing improper behavior
- Unaccustomed freedom (no restraints of parents, school, or employment)
- Lost identity (being dressed in suit and tie, white shirt with short hair, or nylons and conservative dresses, as the case may be)
- Fewer letters from home
- Admiration for "good," likeable people who don't understand your personal values, such as the Word of Wisdom, chastity, and keeping the Sabbath day holy

Ah ha! Satan at work.

When you seem to be losing the battle within, study every

aspect of your life and try to square them up.

Combat damaging temptations by adhering strictly to mission rules, to Church standards, and to personal habits of spiritual growth, such as prayer, cleanliness, scripture study, an attitude of helpfulness to others (including your companion, no matter what).

Seek the confirmation of God's love for you and his abiding interest in the work he has called you to do. It will come. The Lord has promised that if we do what is right and wise by keeping all of His commandments He will encircle us about in the arms of His love. The feeling will be very real and satisfying. Try it and see.

It is your personal mustard seed.

THE BATTLE WITHOUT

Courage. You can win this battle, too, where others may fail, because you know who the enemy is.

You have been given the gift of the Holy Ghost to —

- Protect you
- Warn you
- Inspire you to know right from wrong
- Help you discern evil in designing men and situations
- Allow you to recognize the elements that promote powers of darkness
- Witness to you of Christ, who himself overcame the world, won the battle, and paved the way for us.

With God nothing is impossible. Dr. Henry Eyring, a world class scientist, lived a life of public service, but privately was a disciple of Christ and devoted to Church service. He once advised people to keep personally clean and close to the Lord and to attack life's problems from that vantage point. He gave credit to his own father, who gave him that counsel as he left home for college.

SOME QUESTIONS TO CONSIDER

Do you qualify as somebody trustworthy — somebody with strength to win battles and help others? Consider these questions:

1. If you were choosing someone you had to trust with your life, with your secret, with your love, or with your money, would you choose yourself?

2. If you were looking for help when trouble hit you square on, would you look for someone like you?

3. If you needed someone to arbitrate an important confusion or difference of opinion, would you choose yourself as a fair judge?

4. Would you honor an unwritten agreement as well as a signed contract?

5. Do you care more about what men think than about God's opinion of you?

6. Are you familiar with the questions asked by priesthood authority during the interview for a temple recommend? Could you pass today? Would you feel worthy to interview yourself?

7. If you were looking for a good example of a believer in Christ, would you choose yourself? Can you be counted on to testify of Christ?

May you be victorious in both the battle within yourself and the battle without. Satan wants you to fail. The Savior can help you win.

42

An Inimitable Blessing

If you ever have the opportunity, wander through the halls of Westminster Abbey and listen to the echoing whispers of mankind. There history is revealed through epitaphs etched on stacked tombs, chiseled on floor marbles, marked on wall niches of the dead. Kings of England lie beside common men. Archbishops and warriors sandwich the heartaches of man's move through life. Sinners and saints surround the poets' corner — all are aloof to restraints of time.

Joseph Addison, following his own visit to Westminster for a long look at life, wrote these lines: "When I look upon the tombs of the great, every emotion of envy dies in me; when I read the epitaphs of the beautiful, every inordinate desire goes out; when I meet with the grief of parents upon a tomb-stone, my heart melts with compassion; when I see the tomb of the parents themselves, I consider the vanity of grieving for those whom we must quickly follow: when I seek kings lying by those who deposed them, when I consider rival wits placed side by side, or the holy men that divided the world with their contests and disputes, I reflect with sorrow and astonishment on the little competitions, factions, and debates of mankind. When I read the several dates of the tombs, of some that died yesterday, and some six hundred years ago, I consider the great Day when we shall all of us be contemporaries, and make our appearance together."

This experience inevitably arouses the question of the purpose of life, of how we spend our days, and of what is recorded in our own book of acts.

What are we to do with history's lessons, the probabilities of the future?

What difference can we make in today?

What cause is grand enough for our energies?

What battles are worth fighting and dying for?

What good can be done?

What does today have to do with all the tomorrows?

What do we live and work and die for if not to make the world less difficult for each other?

"God only knows," said one spectator.

If this is true, for our own turn on earth we need to discover what God knows and what his will is for us that our days will not be wasted.

Whatever was the lot of others — in the Garden of Eden, on the ark, crossing the plains, or soaring into space — we are covenant children of God.

We have been called to serve as missionaries. We teach the gospel through which people learn the fulness and goodness of life, by which they understand personal possibilities and joy.

Ours is the inimitable blessing of bringing people to Christ.

For this inimitable blessing we prepare ourselves.

43

Happiness

❝The best two years of my life" is a frequently used phrase at missionary homecoming reports.

Two years of hard work and discipline, self-sacrificing behavior, frustrating days and weeks, living among strangers, forgetting the pleasures of life with loved ones, missing the comforts of home — this sums up to happiness?

Yes!

Happiness does not necessarily correlate with feeling good or being comfortable. Just ask your mother about the day you were born. Ask Jesus about his hours of agony in the garden of Gethsemane when He took upon His own being all the sins and pain of mankind and suffered until blood came through His pores! Shortly thereafter He was ridiculed, tortured, crucified, and died. By dying He rose again to show us that in death there is life. He introduced incredible hope of life everlasting, of reunion and restoration. Christ was definitely not comfortable, but joy was full!

Happiness is not about comfort or getting your own way. Happiness cannot come without doing things God's way!

A word of caution and reminder: Christ said, "For, behold, I, God, have suffered these things for all, that they might not suffer if they would repent, but if they would not repent they must suffer even as I; which suffering caused myself, even God, the greatest of all, to tremble because of pain, and to bleed at every pore, and to suffer both body and spirit — and would that I might not drink the bitter cup, and shrink — nevertheless, glory be to the Father, and I partook and finished my preparations unto the children of men" (D&C 19:16-19).

The missionary who works for the glory of God recognizes that the best two years of his life thus far happened because he was closely following the Savior. The more a person is like the Savior, seeks the will of the Lord, and applies it to life, the more joy of soul he or she will feel. Happiness, then, relates to obedience because certainly wickedness never was happiness.

Happiness is about peace, about loving and being loved, about bringing joy to others, and about being on track with your life in control. Happiness is feeling the approval of God because you are doing what is right and good. Happiness is dependent upon the amount of God's love that you possess and share. The love of God is the most desirable fruit of life. He died for us because He loved us. Incredible! Would you, could you, do this for someone else? Talk that one over with your mother!

The love of Heavenly Father is that He gave us life as well as the plan to live by so we could learn and grow and enjoy. He gave us his Son to change our quality of life and to bring us back home to heaven.

"He doeth not anything save it be for the benefit of the world; for he loveth the world, even that he layeth down his own life that he may draw all men unto them. Wherefore, he commandeth none that they shall not partake of this salvation" (2 Nephi 26:24).

Happiness happens when we apply the atonement of Christ to ourselves, when we take it personally. We choose to accept his gift, to repent and live the Christlike life.

LIVING THE CHRISTLIKE LIFE

Living the Christlike life may mean for you waking up in the morning and saying to yourself, "Whom can I bless this day?"

Instead of saying, "What's in it for me?" you say "What can I do for someone else?" or "How can I further the Lord's work?"

Put yourself second. Hold the door open for someone else. Ask if you can help the handicapped. Allow the other car to take the parking place. Don't race through the yellow light ahead of the turning traffic. Offer to let someone go ahead of you in the ticket line, the check-out line, onto the bus, along the chapel bench, down the aisle.

Keep the commandments with exactness. A mission president received this note from one of the Sister missionaries in his area: "I just wanted to write you a short note to express my gratitude for challenging us a few weeks ago to obey with exactness. I accepted your challenge, and since then I have felt the Spirit more than at any other time in my life. Its influence has been with me almost constantly. I can't thank you enough because of the wonderful blessings that have resulted from the companionship of the Holy Ghost."

Confess and repent. "All those who are proud, and that do wickedly, the day that cometh shall burn them up, saith the Lord of Hosts, for they shall be as stubble...and mountains shall cover them, and whirlwinds shall carry them away.... But behold, the righteous that hearken unto the words of the prophets,...[who] look forward unto Christ with steadfastness for the signs which are given, notwithstanding all persecution — behold, they are they which shall not perish" (2 Nephi 26:4-5, 8). Since we are not perfect, and since happiness depends on Christ-likeness, repentance becomes the way to happiness. "Behold, he who has repented of his sins, the same is forgiven, and I, the Lord, remember them no more. By this ye may know if a man repenteth of his sins — behold, he will confess them and forsake them" (D&C 58:42-43).

Love God. Proof of your love for God and Christ is to control yourself in every situation, to make the mighty effort toward self-mastery. Decide today how you will act in every conceivable situation — in times of imposition, hurt feelings, disagreement, or temptation of any kind. Big problems grow out of little ones left unchecked!

When you seek to live the Christlike life, it at last becomes clear why Christ counseled us to turn the other cheek, to give the cloak as well as the coat, to walk the second mile, to do good unto others. Looking for happiness includes knowing and loving God enough so that we act according to God's will rather than react according to the world.

Pray and serve, teach and baptize, comfort, inspire, and love in secret rather than to be seen by men. When you are seen by men you have your reward! God's glory is ignored. His style is to do things because of someone's need, not for personal enhancement.

Take the example of seeing snow left on a widow's walk. Here's a chance to do a good deed, to help her. You could get up early and shovel when no one else is about. Or you could wait until eight o'clock A.M. when all the neighbors are going to school and to work and they would see you. Of course, you see the point.

What about success with an investigator? The baptism is a glorious moment of bringing people to Christ. Or it can be spoiled with a cavalier attitude: "Hooray, that's four baptisms this month for me!"

Happiness to the missionary is bringing people to Christ. This important time of serving the Lord can be the beginning of a lifetime of happiness by living as He wants us to live. Happiness can be eternity in the presence of God.

44

FUNDAMENTAL
CONSIDERATIONS

There are certain fundamental considerations to teaching
the gospel of Jesus Christ. The First Presidency and the
Council of the Twelve of The Church of Jesus Christ of
Latter-day Saints issued a formal statement on this matter
dated June 1991. It is summarized here (with several direct
quotations from the document) for your convenience, as well
as your edification as a missionary. This focus is the official
standard for proselyting for all the Church on all levels. It is
helpful to find this focus and standard in one place. (Wording
of headings is the same as that used in the document.)

1. *Proclaiming the Gospel.* The Lord is opening doors and
   hastening his work in all the world. "We urge priesthood
   leaders, members, and missionaries to increase their
   efforts, working in unity and faith, so that many more of
   the children of our Father in Heaven will be converted,
   accept His Son, become members of His Church, remain
   steadfast in keeping His commandments, and receive all
   of the ordinances of the temple."

2. *Doctrinal Basis.* The doctrinal foundation for teaching the
   gospel should be strictly adhered to so that errors will be
   avoided and proselyting activities will conform to inspired
   instructions regarding the work. There are significant

scriptures to help. For example, "And again, the elders, priests and teachers of this church shall teach the principles of my gospel, which are in the Bible and the Book of Mormon, in the which is the fulness of the gospel. And they shall observe the covenants and church articles to do them, and these shall be their teachings, as they shall be directed by the Spirit. And the Spirit shall be given unto you by the prayer of faith; and if ye receive not the Spirit ye shall not teach" (D&C 42:12-14).

3. *Missionary Program of the Church.* "The current missionary program of the Church, contained in the missionary discussions, the missionary training guide, and approved training materials, is consistent with the direction given by the Lord and is to be used in training priesthood leaders, members, and missionaries."

4. *Balanced Effort.* "Lives will be blessed more consistently and the growth of the Church sustained more uniformly as we simultaneously emphasize conversion, retention, and activation."

5. *Proper Methods.* "'As part of the preparation for baptism, investigators should —

a. Be taught all of the standard missionary discussions before baptism and have come to a knowledge of the Savior.

b. Have attended regular Sunday church meetings (such as sacrament meeting) and should feel a unity and oneness with church members; and have been introduced to the bishop or branch president.

c. Repent, and thereafter love and serve God with all their hearts, and commit to keeping his commandments.'

"The focus must be to provide for each person who can be encouraged to listen the opportunity to understand and live basic gospel principles so each one, using moral agency, can choose to exercise faith, repent, take upon himself the name of Jesus Christ, and join His Church.

"In their personal preparation, missionaries should concentrate on their spiritual development as well as their proselyting skills."

The Lord has certain requirements that investigators should meet to qualify for baptism: "All those who humble themselves before God, and desire to be baptized, and come forth with broken hearts and contrite spirits, and witness before the church that they have truly repented of all their sins, and are willing to take upon them the name of Jesus Christ, having a determination to serve him to the end, and truly manifest by their works that they have received of the Spirit of Christ unto the remission of their sins, shall be received by baptism into his church" (D&C 20:37).

6. *Missionary Service.* "Priesthood leaders, stake missionaries, and full-time missionaries [should] work as one to help all members experience the joy of missionary service by accepting missionary callings, actively preparing individuals to hear the gospel, and diligently welcoming and fellowshiping new converts."

45

WHEN YOU LEAVE
YOUR FIELD OF LABOR

There are two things to remember about leaving your field of labor as a missionary: (1) return home with honor and (2) have no regrets. The time to think about returning home with honor and without regrets is when you leave for your mission. Start with determination to be the missionary your mission president, your family, your bishop, and your Father in Heaven want you to be. Set your own high standards for performance and for learning the deep value of this rare experience. Then, when it's time to go home, there will be no regrets about not having given your mission time the best you had in you. You will have made yourself available to the Lord and the work. You will have kept the mission rules, established to keep missionaries free from the hamperings of Satan and to keep them constantly striving to walk the straight and narrow path with the companionship of the Holy Ghost.

Going on a mission — whatever your age — is a great foundation for your eternal life that begins afresh with your homecoming. Prepare to succeed in life as well as you did on your mission. Have a clear vision of who you are, who you are about to become, and what you should be about in the real world of good against evil and the mighty struggles of every day.

Set goals and make plans for education, vocation, marriage,

169

and a balanced life, with as much emphasis on spiritual growth as on temporal efforts.

Life can be a grand adventure. After all, life is God-given! Live with a desire to drink deeply of its joys and challenges. The details of each person's life will be different. Often life doesn't turn out to be what you thought it would be. But remember, God is at the helm. Remember that, and you'll find the wonderful surprises he has in store for you.

Work at being the best you possibly can be — a special "no limit" kind of thinker and doer. Work with all your soul so that when you finish your life's mission you can return to meet your Heavenly Father with honor and no regrets.

46

ALL THE REST OF YOUR LIFE

The missionary arrived home four days after Christmas, and his family waited to celebrate the day with him. The day of their Christmas began as usual with family prayer. Everyone knelt in a circle, and the father of the family prayed. Soon it was clear that somebody was weeping. What was the trouble? Their missionary was home, and Christmas was at hand! The mother knows her child, even when he has been away for two years. She realized that it was the missionary himself who was weeping, and in her heart she felt his "homesickness in reverse." He missed the people he'd left behind in Germany. He loved his family, and he was glad to be home, but in the mission field he had become a man. His extended relationships were hard won, gospel touched, God blessed. And he wept for what had been and would never quite be again.

Coming home after a mission has all the scent of Wordsworth's poetry in which he speaks of earthly birth as our coming from another sphere "trailing clouds of glory." Think of all the wonder that can happen during a mission — closeness to Christ in a way the missionary simply may never have realized was possible; fasting and yearning and hoping over near strangers as they carefully step ever closer to baptism; silently praying for guidance to know what to say in a teaching situation. After all, just the right phrase, the right spirit could assist the investigator toward the font. Fasting and praying to overcome homesickness, personal sin, discouragement, companion clashes, procrastination in scripture study, doors that don't open on any street, cultural shock-strengths are born in crises and difficulties that will carry the returned missionary throughout his or her life.

One day, after more fasting and praying, the missionary reaches the turning point! Nothing really changes, but everything is different. The Spirit swells, the restless heart is stilled Whatever was hard before is hard yet, but like the bitter cup that was drunk, glorious things happened. Suddenly that mission is the happiest time of that missionary's life — new perspectives, life changers, experiences that deepen feelings, wonderful happenings that firm a testimony, struggles that prove the worth in character.

Now, home.

Reentry.

Family prayer with people you love — same names, same relationships, but strangers nonetheless. Reunion with friends who march to a different trump. You are in their world but not of it. They coax, "Come off it." Will you or won't you?

How do you go about living the former life with new values?

Heavenly Father has helped you before when you entered the mission field. He will help you again now that you are home. You can carefully, thoughtfully make the transition from fulltime service to a productive life of school, work, marriage, retirement — whatever is your real life now.

But keep those special months of service as the standard by which you will live. Don't waste them by tossing aside the great new habits learned. These should be part of your life forever. Preparing to go on a mission is preparing for all the rest of your life, here and hereafter. Here are twelve suggestions about returning home to ponder before you ever leave!

CALLED TO SERVE HIM

1. Get a temple recommend and keep it current. Use it often. Wear your special clothing properly and in gratitude for sacred covenants with God.

2. Give pure thanks out of a full heart in your daily prayer. Blessing counting draws you closer, ever closer, to the giver of all good things in life. Remember that Heavenly Father and the Lord Jesus Christ pour out blessings upon you, not because you are so great, but because they are.

3. Remember daily personal prayer on your knees in true humility as you gently ask God's help to know his will; to receive his forgiveness because you have slipped from your goals, sinned, or been selfish; to receive God's blessing upon you for the strength to endure, resist, perform, and serve.

4. Study the Book of Mormon for a certain period every day. Your mission schedule provided such study time. When you are home you must find your own protected time. You'll be struggling with the hectic schedule of living in a world that provides traffic lights, police protection, fire safety, public schools, and IRS forms, but there is no law about a set time for spiritual growth.

5. Write in your journal, and review it regularly. At least a line or two every day is a good habit and keeps you obedient. It reminds you of your best times and God's answers to your prayers. Keep your long-range as well as short-term goals ever before you.

6. Have a blessing on every meal, even if you are in a public place and you pray privately and silently. A proper blessing to ask of Heavenly Father includes gratitude for the food and a blessing that it may be pure and good for your body. Missionaries come up against some strange food in strange places where standards are not as high as required by United States Food and Drug laws. Pray also that you may use your strength well in your call to serve Him.

7. Find a way to resist temptation by gritting your teeth, doubling your fists, and getting yourself out of the situation (like Joseph of Egypt). Meanwhile read the scriptures or sing a special hymn, like "More Holiness Give Me." What a good song! Memorize and think about all the words. Find ways to appropriately relax, renew, refresh, and recreate that "holiness" feeling within you. Find a way to meditate upon the wonder of being a servant of the Lord and filling your place in his kingdom.

8. Do a kind deed, an act of service. Or surprise someone with a supporting comment, an encouraging word.

9. Determine the point beyond which you will not go to keep a friend, have some fun, earn some money, or get a sweetheart. If you have to compromise your standards, you are traveling in the wrong lane toward a goal unworthy of one who answered the call to serve Him.

10. Keep in touch with your mission president and your choice companions.

11. Accept a Church calling and give it your very best. It will be different from a full-time mission, but it is still serving in the kingdom of God on earth.

12. Honor your father and your mother that your days may be long and your sleep peaceful and untroubled.

And now, may you always remember the blessings that come, the guidance you get, the joy you feel — and can feel all the rest of your life as you respond to the calls to serve Him.

One of the greatest secrets of missionary work is work! If a missionary works, he will get the Spirit; if he gets the Spirit, he will teach by the Spirit; and if he teaches by the Spirit, he will touch the hearts of the people and he will be happy. There will be no home-sickness, no worrying about families, for all time and talents and interests are centered on the work of the ministry. Work, work, work — there is no satisfactory substitute, especially in missionary work.

— Ezra Taft Benson
March 1986